Contact Centre

Recruitment and Retention

A Practical Guide

Kenny Gow

Copyright 2024 – All rights reserved.

For Ann and Jenny.

Chapter 1

Not so long ago I was asked by my then employer - a major UK outsourcing organisation - to support a review of their existing customer service agent recruitment process.

Unsustainably high levels of agent turnover meant that some campaigns were struggling to maintain the numbers of staff required to achieve contractual service levels and to deliver the high standard of service demanded by client companies' customers. Needless to say, my employers were equally concerned about the high cost of having to continually recruit and train such large numbers of new people and were beginning to worry that their hard won strong reputation within the local community was being eroded as so many of the town's people joined the organisation only to leave within a few weeks apparently disillusioned by what they had experienced at our hands.

As a senior operations manager, my input around what my managers were experiencing at the coal face would inform and influence whatever direction the business should decide to take next – assuming we were all agreed that taking a new direction would be the appropriate next step.

A group of senior figures from our Human Resources, Recruitment, Learning/Development, Operations and Resource Planning teams were tasked with pulling apart every aspect of our existing end to end processes and replacing them with something much more 'fit for purpose' that would drive our agent recruitment efforts throughout the 2020s and beyond. The remit was simple: develop and implement a joined-up approach to recruitment, onboarding, induction training, grad bay, go-live and ongoing floor management that delivered above industry average staff retention rates while supporting new hires to achieve their career aspirations within our business in a way that further enhances our reputation as an employer of choice within the local area. Simple!!

We were given three months to complete the task after which we would present our proposals to the board of directors at an away day. Our Director of HR acted as sponsor and we were allocated project management support to help keep us on track. We were permitted to meet as often as the workload required and every technical facility at the organisation's disposal would be made available to us.

I'll refer to this project repeatedly throughout this book as what I learned and experienced during my participation has influenced and underlined a great deal of the methodology I now advocate and advance to others as 'best practice' in the field of recruiting and retaining customer service agents in a modern contact centre environment – irrespective of whether they are employed in primarily voice, chat or social media centric roles.

What follows is a practical step by step guide to developing a bespoke system for hiring, developing and hanging onto the most suitable new recruits to your business. Everything I'm proposing has been tried, tested and produced above average results consistently over the last few years. Apply the guidance enthusiastically and consistently and I'm convinced you will see marked improvement across many aspects of the first 100 days 'journey' of your new hires at agent level leading to lower rates of staff turnover together with higher staff satisfaction scores in your all-important annual SSAT surveys.

As in my other books I have deliberately used a casual writing style suited, I believe, to discussing 'real world' situations where people's emotions and behaviours don't always appear rational and thought-through. I'll refer to customer service agents of all types as CSAs, advisers, consultants and use 'he' or 'she' freely without implying anything gender specific. Team managers may be a TM or TL and Operations Managers as Ops Managers or OMs. I'll freely swap HR for Human Resources or Personnel and a Training department may become 'L and D' if I feel like it.....it's all about avoiding repetition. I'm also very inconsistent in my use of capital letters when naming roles. Sorry but that's the way it is.

It's my habit to apply a very basic and informal Pareto analysis to situations where priorities have to be determined quickly and will often offer lists of three or five activities where I believe you should target your focus for best effect. You'll see that a lot over the next few chapters.

Finally, we owe it to the people who have taken the brave decision to apply to join our organisations to deliver, for them, the best possible experience which supports their hopes and aspirations for the future. I don't have all the answers but I hope that every reader can take away from this book at least one idea or principle that will help to make that decision a profitable one for both the applicant and businesses alike.

So, let's get on with it.....why do people leave our organisations in the first place? Did we do something wrong? Why not ask them?

Chapter 2

If you Google something like 'Why do staff leave call centres?' you'll be bombarded with suggestions of websites run by training and technology companies looking to supply the customer service industry with all it could ever need to run the most informed, educated and technologically capable state of the art equipped contact centres known to man or woman.

Very often these businesses will have commissioned research and reports relating to the most challenging aspects of managing an efficient and effective centre. They then make the research available to customer service organisations free of charge in return for an opportunity to market their wares directly to a person of influence within the interested party. Contact Centre industry on-line magazines may also publish these reports giving the original commissioners free exposure and advertising. Some of this material can prove pretty useful but much will simply trot out the same old headlines about high agent turnover being due to low pay, insufficient training or development opportunities, poor job 'fit', lack of recognition, unsustainable shifts, poor management etc........none of which is inaccurate but, for our purposes, doesn't really help us identify <u>exactly</u> why so many seemingly capable, enthusiastic and ambitious new hires walk out the doors of our centres for the last time having completed less than 2 months service (in some organisations 30% don't even make it out of induction training!!!).

It's useful to find out from the people who stayed on after induction training and went on to enjoy their contact centre careers why they didn't make a swift exit out the door at the first sense that the role wasn't all going to be sweetness and light. Why did they persevere when others threw in the towel? Many suppliers to the industry will commission this kind of research as well and some of the top level information can act as useful pointers.

My point is this: if you want to reduce staff turnover you must first find out the real reasons why leavers <u>really</u> left your business in the first place. For this exercise to be truly useful it's crucial to narrow your focus to how localised conditions impact on an employee's decision to leave a new job just a few weeks into a tenure which both parties had believed would be a great deal longer and more successful at outset.

So, where do you find this information?

This was one of the first questions we asked ourselves when we set up our review project team. It was clear early on that, as a business, we didn't really have the clearest view on why we were losing so many new staff early in their tenure. Like most similar organisations we kept extensive records of the 'leaver's interviews' performed by line managers when one of their direct reports gives notice to leave the company. These are useful in as much as the information and opinions gleaned would often provide a snapshot of how someone who, on the whole, would be moving on to a new job with a rival employer or into full-time education, felt about a number of key aspects of our customs, practices and general culture.

We also had the results of our most recent annual staff satisfaction survey which, though disappointing, hadn't been entirely surprising. In fact they almost exactly mirrored the previous two years' numbers and comments relating to how staff felt we, as a business, were doing in terms of developing our staff and keeping them happy while in the building. The top five concerns of our people across three years were:

- Pay/Salary
- Training and Development
- Promotion Opportunities
- Management Style and Approach
- Unsocial Hours/Shifts

It shouldn't be a surprise to anyone that these were also the main reasons given by those who participated in exit or leavers interviews before moving on to new jobs elsewhere. If I were someone who had performed well in my role over a number of months I would be looking for my line manager to support me in further developing my skills and in finding a new opportunity within the organisation. When it looks like these things aren't happening most people will look outside the business for an advanced and better paid opportunity – perhaps a role that didn't involve working two full weekends in every three thus allowing for a better work/life balance.

The company had taken all of the satisfaction survey feedback on-board and had been working to improve salaries and bonuses. 'Academy' style classes for our elite performers with potential to move into management, IT, HR or L and D had been created and we constantly reviewed shift patterns and our full-time/part-time mix of staff to try to build the improved work/life balance every long-standing contact centre agent and team manager dreams about. For many, these changes were happening too slowly and decided to take advantage of the recent opening of a competitor's centre just a couple of miles up the road from us and move on. There was little – other than offer promises of good things to come – that we could do to prevent our best (and some who weren't quite as good as they thought they were) from making the move elsewhere.

It was clear that improvements weren't happening quickly enough but we were certain that we were on the correct path and that we would ultimately deliver a package that would compete with our noisy neighbours on the other side of town. But what of the people who joined us and then left within ninety days or less? Surely their reasons for moving on would be different from those listed by our more experienced people? It was crucial that we find that out but what was the best way of going about that? These people had all already left us and we weren't in a position to talk to them about why they'd changed their minds about us so early in their careers. We required a strategy that would deliver the exact reasons why we didn't meet the standards set by our newest people. How could we get to the bottom of this fundamental issue?

For me, as an Operations Manager, the immediate priority was the obvious 90 day leaver issue. Why were so many new recruits leaving before the end of their probation period having recently joined us keen to start a career filed with enthusiasm and excitement? As many as 50% of all new customer service adviser staff were resigning before the end of their first three months with us. Most of them didn't offer formal resignations and simply disappeared into the night never to be seen again. What was causing these people to make that decision?

It was always going to be a challenge to get to speak to recent leavers who failed to follow the recognised leaving process. They may be embarrassed by their actions or angry about how they felt they had been treated. They may be worried that we could be chasing them for overpayment of wages or to ask for return of equipment or training materials. It's fair to say that they wouldn't be in a hurry to speak to us. So, how should we go about getting them to help us to get to the bottom of one of the biggest issues our business was facing? Also, how could we use our existing staff to give us an accurate picture of what it is like to be recruited, trained and employed by our organisation? Many new recruits had been recommended to us by existing staff as part of a 'Refer a Friend' scheme. This meant that employees would receive a cash bonus if they put forward a family member or friend for a new customer service role and that person subsequently successfully completed training and probation. The guys who had done the recommending would surely have some insight into why their friends had left the job so suddenly – how could we get them to share this without causing any form of recrimination aimed either at the leaver or the business? A pretty sensitive task to be honest.

What about relatively new staff who had successfully completed training and probation and were now regarded as settled staff members? I was pretty sure they would have some views on why so many new recruits they had trained alongside left before going live on the floor and what we could do to prevent this happening in future. So, let's ask them but make sure we do it in a 'safe' environment where they can speak freely and directly to senior executives without the presence of the recruiters, trainers and managers who had played a part in bringing them on board in the first place. If well controlled, so much can be learned from 'skip level' meetings where a senior manager sits down over a buffet lunch with staff she would not normally come into contact with and speaks about the concerns of these employees without their line managers being present.

Having broken the entire process down into the key functions we called simply advertising, recruitment, training, nursery and go-live it was decided that we would focus our fact-finding on these to begin with. It seemed very likely that a more complex range of sub-headings would evolve during the exercise and that our focus would change as a result. In the meantime we would keep it as simple as possible for all concerned. Our initial objective would be to discover all that was 'good' and 'bad' about how we advertised the customer service role, the current recruitment process, our training and trainers, the soft live process and ultimately what it's like to successfully complete all the initial stages then be released into 'the wild' as part of an existing team of experienced staff managed by a team manager unknown to you.

A word of warning – these 'let's get to the bottom of things' type of exercises are never much fun for people working in the departments most likely to suffer criticism as a result. Most people I know work really hard and put their heart and soul into making the work of their unit as effective as possible. To publicly be told that what you've been throwing yourself into day after day for months isn't well regarded and must change significantly can be a slap in the face and all parties involved must engage in the process with care and sensitivity and in the knowledge that the finger of blame may well be pointed at everyone at some point in the process. It's pretty fair to say that, if 50% of staff leave their new jobs within three months, they are going to be critical of some of the people who recruited, trained and managed them in the short time they were employed. Believe me when I say that those who leave before completing training will almost certainly blame your organisation and some of the people in it for deciding to pack their things and go and find something else. Almost no-one we spoke to felt strong enough to say they weren't capable of seeing things through to a successful conclusion...they all believed that their failure was down to something that someone else in the business had said or done.

So, in summary, we agreed that we would ask three distinct groups a series of fundamental questions designed to help us understand what it was that we were currently doing that made some new recruits decide that they did not want to continue in the role. We would look for the kind of very specific detail that would support a Six Sigma style re-design of existing functions and processes with a view to creating a brand new end-to-end staff attraction, development and retention programme that would signal to existing and potential employees (and our competitors) that we have moved with and ahead of the times and that we were becoming a business fit for the mid-2020s and beyond. We would genuinely put supportive, emotionally intelligent staff recruitment and management at the heart of everything we planned to do going forward.

So, we decided that Stage One would be to email and text 250 individuals who had joined us in the last year, then left within 45 days – and ask them to answer a series of simple but insightful questions regarding their time with us and relating to their reasons why they felt they couldn't continue their careers with us. We kept the questionnaire as short as possible and offered shopping gift vouchers as a reward to those who responded and gave us their postal address. In the end, we received 32 responses. Some were helpful while others gave us nothing to move forwards with. We responded with approximately £500 in gift vouchers which we'd already purchased for use as incentives so, other than postage, there was no additional cost to the business.

Should you go down the route of emulating this kind of exercise it's really important that you don't expect too much from it. There will be a few nuggets of gold in there somewhere but please don't hope for too much insight into where it's all been going wrong. The overall, generalised response formed part of our total, final report but gave us little to support wholesale changes in what our recruitment had looked like up until that point.

As you would imagine, Pay/Salary and Promotion Opportunities didn't really feature: none of these guys were in the business long enough for either of these concerns to become prominent in their thinking. Unsuitable Working Hours, on the other hand, had been a major concern for most. Verbatim comments noted that many leavers had convinced themselves that they would manage to fit their lives around the times we required them to be in the building but, in the end, this had proved impossible to sustain due to family and on-going social commitments.

Frankly, this isn't really what we wanted to hear as we were only too aware how difficult it would be to change existing shift patterns while remaining cost-efficient. It quickly became clear that, if we couldn't change the existing shift patterns, we would have to be much more certain that potential recruits were made aware of the challenges of constantly working on these shifts and build individual, bespoke plans that ensured new staff had contingency in place to deliver their committed hours irrespective of what family and social challenges they were presented with as their careers progressed. In short, we would have to take them through the complex , unexpected life events that would be likely to show themselves then form detailed 'adverse event' procedures that would fall into place as and when the issues inevitably showed up. I'll cover this in more detail later but want to emphasise at this point that this is the kind of thinking you'll have to get used to when you hit brick wall situations – if a 'fundamental' aspect of running the centre cannot be changed then you must come up with effective action plans designed to offset the worst of the implications of keeping a fundamental in situ.

Next most frequent reason for leaving we were given was that 'The Job Just wasn't For Me'. This meant that some joiners had a view of the job wasn't accurate or that they knew exactly what the day-to-day looked and felt like but couldn't bring themselves to tolerate the relative volatility and disciplines that form essential parts of the Customer Service Agent Role. Many responders said that they had under-estimated the extent to which customers can be both demanding and negative leaving the call handler with feelings of ineptitude and constantly being ineffective. The repetitive element of the role also got some of the new staff down. They believed that the job would be more varied and stimulating than they discovered it actually was. Had they stayed with us a little longer they would have learned that contact centres offer a greater variety of roles and responsibilities than many other working environments but we never got the chance to demonstrate this to those who left us as early as this group did. This was clearly an area we could do better at advertising, recruitment and training stages.

Next on the list of reasons why expensive new recruits left us within the first few weeks was lack of confidence in induction training. Almost all responders stated that they felt our initial training was insufficient to allow them to do their best for customers as they went live. Almost everyone who responded to the survey concluded that they were not ready to handle live calls when they came out of training and that the course had focussed on parts of the job that were irrelevant. Now, we all know that no-one feels ready to handle live calls when they first move from Training to Grad Bay and I'm not sure how we, as an industry, fully overcome that. However, most new recruits who feel that way stay with us and go on to become pillars of our business. I wanted to know why our 'pillars' stayed with us while the early leavers made a totally different decision in exactly the same circumstances and what we could do to help the latter group understand that they will succeed and begin to enjoy the role if they simply push through the initial doubts that all new staff experience.

Next, and possibly related to what I've just written, was the general feeling that they weren't given enough support when they went live for the first time. Many stated that our Grad Bay management team had been initially helpful and understanding but that they became noticeably more intolerant as the days passed – to the extent that some new trainees became nervous of raising their hands and asking for help on challenging calls leading to some trainees trying to muddle through on their own and probably creating the kind of minor mess that would result in repeat calls, unhappy customers, complaints together with time being wasted having to require experienced staff to fix the issues created by our newest people.

As we had taken great care in selecting both the managers and support staff working on Grad Bay it was disappointing to learn that some new staff felt that these hand-chosen people had become unsympathetic, lacking in empathy and, in some cases, downright unhelpful. We checked this out when we later spoke to our newest staff who had gone on to make a success of their roles and, thankfully, the picture was much brighter. The people within this group believed that Grad Bay staff had been both supportive and helpful and none felt that the team had become unapproachable in any way. We recognised, of course, that not everyone felt so positive about the post-induction support they had received so we designed an updated training/re-training course for the Grad Bay staff which included references to the negative feedback received with instruction and discussion around how to minimise the potential for any of our new people to feel that they should leave their new role due to lack of empathetic support.

Needless to say, the Grad Bay team were quick to offer their own points of view on why a number of leavers had blamed them for their ultimate decision to leave their roles. Almost all expressed frustration that a few new trainees simply didn't listen to the help and advice they were offered and repeatedly asked the same questions around how to handle the most straight forward of calls. Some even suggested that a handful of trainees were so disinterested that no amount of side-by-side mentoring would get them to a place that we could be confident they could be left to their own devices when handling calls. We also received feedback that a small number of inductees had such poor communication and PC skills that only highly intensive, time consuming, focussed development would get them to the point where they could handle calls without constant supervision. It was apparent that some new recruits were squeezing through our selection process without the necessary basic skills required to make a decent fist of the job and that we would have to stiffen up our initial testing to reduce the likelihood of people who would simply never reach the minimum standards required to be effective in the CSA position.

Next issue consistently raised was the general attitude of Team Managers and quality of support offered when new trainees went live having successfully left Grad Bay. Too many times complaints were being raised around how insensitive and unhelpful experienced staff were when recent trainees joined their teams. We heard stories of managers simply ignoring the new recruits on their first day live leaving them to struggle through calls unsupported leading to repeat calls and complaints from customers when unhappy with the standard of customer service being offered. New agents spoke of Team Managers and experienced staff showing a lack of empathy and, in some cases, complete disinterest. This left the newbies to feel exposed and irrelevant and unable to make meaningful connections with their new colleagues.

It appeared that no effort was made to allow our inductees to take scheduled breaks and lunches at the same times as the people they had got to know while in training leaving them to wander around the building on their own looking for a familiar face or, as in a couple of cases, to lock themselves away in their cars in the car park failing to engage with anyone in the business who could help them feel at home from an early point in their careers with us. It's clear to see how this would lead to some of our recent trainees becoming lonely and disheartened.

As you can imagine, all of this feedback made my blood boil. Having spent a total of £2k+ in recruiting and training each of these individuals and having arranged for them to be fully supported when going live after Grad Bay, I could see no reason why this could possibly become an area for employees to tell us that we had let them down and contributed to their reasons for leaving. Needless to say, the Team managers we had selected to take responsible for new graduates had a great deal to say about the feedback we had received from leavers.

I brought each of the responsible managers together for a group wash-up session covering how successful they had felt in supporting the members of their team who had left the business within three months of joining us. I requested that they brought all the relevant paperwork with them which could support their views; I was pleased to see that all TMs had evidence of coaching, 121s and formal conversations to back up what they had to tell me.

In summary, this group was pretty clear on the reasons why we had lost the new team members within such a short timescale and had a very clear perspective on what we could do to avoid leaving ourselves in this kind of position going forwards. In no particular order they were:

- *Insufficient training and Grad Bay experience*
- *Unwillingness to learn how to deal with calls on their own*
- *Inability to work scheduled shifts*
- *Reluctance to mix with new team members*
- *Poor PC skills*
- *Overall disinterest* In almost all cases managers claimed that they could identify from an early stage who would form part of the 90 day leavers group and, irrespective of the support they offered, very little could have been done to to persuade them to stay. A belief had developed within the business that at least two people in every group of 15 who joined us had pre-determined that they would only be

staying with us for a matter of weeks and their motivation for taking the roles in the first place was to mollify family members or the government's Department of Social Security who had been putting pressure on them to get into some kind of work or risk losing key state benefits. We had no formal evidence that this was the case but some managers claimed that the subject had been raised by new staff during informal conversations. Our HR department were able to show us communications from the benefits office received almost immediately after our leavers had handed in their resignations or simply left the business without any form of notice. I guess this backs up the notion that an early departure followed by an immediate benefits claim may have been on at least some of these guys' minds during their time with us. For me, however, it outlined a belief I'd had for some time that some new staff join us with little or no notion that they would be under pressure to do the job well once they had settled in and that we would not just be happy with people who turned up regularly but made no effort to be effective in the role. This was clearly something we would have to cover with applicants at the earliest stages of recruitment and test for throughout induction.

Now, you might think we were not really making much progress at this point; after all, for every point raised by a leaver there was a counter point raised by the Team Manager community alongside training and Grad Bay people. In fact, this was exactly what I'd been hoping to receive. Surely, if we could make the kinds of changes which would all but guarantee happier outcomes on both sides of the equation we would all be in a better place? That was always the plan.

Next, I wanted to hear what our existing CSR community had to say on the subject. Why did some people persevere and go on to build a career with us while others jumped ship at the first sign of discomfort?

Chapter 3

It was crucially important for management to hear the views of our successful agents on the subject of why most new trainees went on to succeed in their roles – to a greater or lesser extent - while others left the business at the first sign of things not turning out as they had hoped.

I arranged for a series of 'skip level' meetings to take place where enthusiastic, intelligent and mouthy members of the agent community could freely express their opinions on the subjects of advertising, interviews, training, Grad Bay and going 'live' on the floor in their designated teams. These types of meetings are known as 'skip level' as managers and their supporting supervisors are not asked to attend allowing their direct reports to express themselves freely and without fear of any sort or repercussions. If you want to understand how your staff are really feeling about their roles, workplace and managers then you have to give them free reign to speak as they wish with a cast iron guarantee that nothing specific will get back to the ears of their bosses.

If you plan to run such sessions please be advised that you have to have absolute control of the terms of reference and planned topics of discussion. A rod of iron will be required to keep the meetings on track as almost every attendee will want to air their personal grievances which will range from the lack of oat milk in the café through parking issues at the busiest times of day and onto complaints about the way senior managers distance themselves from the floor and the agent community in general. As facilitator it will be your role to gently steer the group back onto the matters in hand –

recruitment and retention – while acknowledging concerns raised relating to other workplace supposed issues. Be warned, if you get the balance wrong you will have irritated some of your key employees and damaged the value of similar future interactions.

To help start things off on the correct foot I used to introduce the sessions like this:

Thanks for coming along today to give me the benefit of your views on a couple of matters that are becoming increasingly important to the business as we move into the next stage of our development. Each of you has been specially selected as we believe you may have valuable insight to share that can help us to improve in areas where we may be falling behind in how we go about recruiting, training and hanging onto our best people. In fact, I see you as being amongst our best people so I'd love to hear your opinions on how we attract and retain more who are just like you. You have free reign to speak as you wish without making personal remarks about fellow staff members and no relevant criticism is out of bounds. We only have an hour to capture all of your opinions so I would really appreciate it if you could focus exclusively on how we recruit, train and keep our people. I know you'll be tempted to raise things like parking, the food in the café, cleanliness of the toilets etc. and I promise we will pick these concerns in a future session. Please forgive me if I come across as abrupt when pulling us back to the topics in hand. I don't meant to be harsh, its just that I'm nervous of us running out of time. Is everyone ok with that?

Great, please grab a plate and help yourself to sandwiches and snacks and we'll kick off in five minutes exactly. Any questions?

Needless to say we'd only be five minutes in to the session before someone would raise an issue that wasn't strictly relevant and I'd have to pull the conversation back on track...people get a little carried away in these sessions as it's often the very first time they've been offered the opportunity to let off steam to a senior manager without any fear of retribution from their own immediate superior. On that subject, it's inevitable that the TMs will want to hear from you about how the sessions had panned out. It is absolutely crucial that you do not offer any critical feedback of their direct reports and deliver only a positive overview of the information gleaned from the agent group. Let me assure you that if you do anything else the managers will go back to their people and imply that you had in some way been critical of attendees or hadn't taken their opinions seriously. Be the wisest person in the room and keep your views on individuals to yourself.

So, with the help of our HR generalist partner taking notes I asked the group if they were happy for me to record the session on my phone to allow us to capture all of their thoughts as we didn't want to miss anything. They were happy as long as I didn't share the recording with Team Managers and agreed that we would spend twenty minutes discussing each area in detail – i.e. recruitment, training, graduate bay or nursery and going live in teams. We would dedicate twenty minutes to each then have a wash-up or wrap-up at the end when I would take them through the proposed next steps. I informed them that I was interested in their own opinions based on their own experiences but that I was also keen to hear about anyone who had joined as on a recommendation of an existing member of staff but who subsequently left. Why did they leave ? What was it about the role or the business that wasn't to their taste? What did they believe we could have done differently? First, recruitment.

Recruitment

It had long been our practice to advertise CSA roles in local and national newspapers and on local radio. Applicants would complete an on-line form. After consideration, successful applicants would be contacted by our recruitment team to arrange a telephone interview. If that went well a further face-to-face or Zoom/Teams final competency-based interview would take place with the most suitable applicants being offered a role via Email within five working days.

Instructions would be given around bringing identification, passports, visas, utility bills etc. on a given morning before formal induction training was due to begin. Contracts would be signed at that point and all new staff would receive a written description of the nature of the role together with very clear details of expected shift patterns and holidays/leave. They would be encouraged to contact our recruitment team ahead of the start of training should they have any relevant questions. Needless to say, after the signing of contracts there would inevitably be a bunch of successful applicants who would suddenly remember that they had booked a holiday or had to attend a wedding or other family occasion either during the planned three week training programme or just after. This is always particularly annoying as we made sure to ask questions about planned holidays during the initial telephone interview in an effort to rule out anyone who simply couldn't meet the attendance requirements within the first six weeks as it's essential to complete training in full then immediately put what's been learned into practice in nursery if a new adviser is to become competent quickly. Still, we have learned over the years that people behave differently when they are applying for a job and are prone to play down any expectations of required time off until after the contract has been signed.

It is also common for recruits to tell us that, having studied the required shift pattern that they may not be able to commit to working, for example, one full weekend and two part weekends in every four week rotation. Or that a 23.00 finish is impossible as they have discovered that the last bus back to their part of town is now at 22.30 and they don't have access to private transport to get them home after that time. I'm pleased to say that we've reduced this sort of behaviour dramatically of late by insisting that anyone successful at telephone interview stage should rule themselves out at that point – very much before the next stage of recruitment – on the grounds that shifts are unsuitable as absolutely no exceptions can be made at a later date. Everyone must be available to work the planned shift rotation in 100% of instances. Interviewers have been instructed to push really hard on this topic as a little effort at interview stage prevents misunderstandings later in the process. Sadly, however, we still get people telling us late in the training or grad bay part of the process that they have 'discovered' that they are unable to work the planned shift pattern and we have had to let them go at that point having wasted a great deal of money bringing them into the business and paying them whilst being trained. You simply cannot make exceptions so early in a new employees career unless you want to be inundated with hundreds of shift change requests from both new and existing staff when they learn that you have set a precedent. Multiple shift changes will lead to scheduling inefficiencies that may end up costing your business a lot of money. If you can afford it and you're convinced it leads to happier and more settled staff then go ahead but you must build the cost into your business model.

I once worked in a centre where we had agreed fifty-nine separate shift patterns amongst just over 400 staff. We had very low attrition (staff turnover) but the scheduling complexity drove our Resource Planning team mad and the whole thing made recruitment more challenging as they battled to cover gaps left when people were on leave or when they left the business. It's hard enough to get the balance right between full and part-time staff without incorporating another fifty or so personalised shift rotations.

Anyway, to return to the sessions we had with experienced advisers. I outlined as simply as I could the existing recruitment process and asked for feedback on whether the group felt it had worked for them. As you can imagine, the floodgates opened as everyone wanted to have their say on where it hadn't been fully effective in their experience. I've listed below the five main areas where they felt we really should be doing better. Here were many more that this five but we had to use a basic Pareto analysis to narrow things down to where we believed we could have the most impact.

1. **The job is not as was described at any point during recruitment or training.** Almost all attendees believed that no attempt was made to describe the day-to-day actuality of the role and that the difficult, complex and, at times, upsetting nature of the work came as a real shock to they system as they began to go live. They believed that they had been 'sold' the position as simply working on the billing queries line for a well-known utilities company handling common payment and bill-related queries from usually satisfied customers when the reality is actually very much more challenging.
2. **A good standard of computer related skills and experience is an absolute requirement.** Again, it

was felt that this area was 'brushed over' at interview and that many trainees became frustrated and angry when training and grad bay staff lost patience with the new people who simply didn't have the IT abilities required to learn the role quickly and effectively.

3. **Interviewers did not cover off the absolute nature of the shift rotation pattern at any point during interview.** Some felt that they were given the impression that they could request a shift change once training was complete and that core shifts were only for those employees who felt that they were manageable. Also, some were told that they should take proposed holiday leave up with their trainer once they joined induction rather than worry about it at recruitment stage. At no point was this mentioned as a possible deal-breaker and that a postponement of start date could be arranged. It felt like every new trainee had been told a different set of facts regarding our flexibility around shifts and shift changes.

4. **No mention was made of the upselling and debt recovery aspects of the role:** A fundamental element of the job has always been to encourage customers to continue their relationship with our client company after they moved home. So, when a customer called to tell us they were moving home, we would note this then ask the caller to agree that we would supply energy to their new property and ask them to settle their current outstanding bill by credit or debit card. Agents would be targeted on both of these from when they go live and these numbers would represent fundamental KPIs when monthly and annual performance was being measured. Needless to say, almost every member of

the agent community we interviewed believed that these parts of the job were never covered at the point of recruitment and that targets were definitely not discussed. Some even claimed that they wouldn't have applied for the job had they known that these kinds of pressures would be applied so early in their time with us.

5. **Almost every aspect of the job was, in fact, different to how things were described at interview:** What emerged from all of the sessions was the feeling that the HR/Recruitment staff who acted as interviewers didn't really have a grasp of what the job entailed and that only mid-way through induction training did trainees begin to understand some of the challenges they would have to face. Many believed that this was the point at which some new staff began to consider leaving the business or vowing that they would indeed leave if the actual working environment became too pressurised or uncomfortable.

Much of this feedback was a little disappointing but not, to be absolutely honest with you, a total surprise to me. I had heard such things in passing on a number of occasions and had attempted to persuade the relevant department to change some of their methods. I was also only too aware that painting a picture of too challenging a role to new trainees meant that we would negatively impact the numbers of people we would be able to persuade to join us from every round of recruitment leaving us in a position where we would have to work ever harder just to recruit basic numbers for our CSA courses. Finding the balance between encouraging new people to join us while giving applicants a thoroughly honest picture of the difficulties of the role is a hard balance to achieve. While it's clearly essential to paint an accurate picture of how the job feels when you're doing it it has to be borne in mind that new agents will begin to feel they can achieve more and more as they gain experience and become more comfortable as part of the team. Too much 'frightening' information at the front of the recruitment process can result in people who would otherwise become successful in their role feeling overwhelmed resulting in their rejection of any job offer we may make to them.

Next we discussed the three week induction training course and how it might be improved. I'll cover the planned improvements in the next part of the book so will just detail the agents' concerns at this point.

1. **The course only covered a small number of the call types the department received:** Six months before the first of these sessions we had analysed all of our call types and arranged them under suitable headings to allow call-handlers to capture this for data management and planning purposes at a later date. We identified fifty-three distinct varieties of call which was far too many for our purposes so we reduced this to fifteen by forcing some types under headings which only just covered the callers reason for contacting us. Of those fifteen we discovered that approximately 80% fell under five main headings and we decided to focus our induction training on these types of call alone. The purpose of this was to simplify the information being delivered to inexperienced staff whilst giving them the best chance of handling the most common call types effectively from day one. The focus group agents felt that this make a certain amount of sense but left nervous trainees dreading a customer requesting something that they had no knowledge of. Our

intention had always been that, in the unlikely event that a newbie would receive a rare call type, they could simply raise their hand and ask the Grad Bay support staff to take them through how to handle the call professionally This would support the customer and educate the new trainee on what to do when that kind of query raised surfaced in the future. Focus session attendees did not believe that this worked for call handlers however as very often no Grad Bay support was available when hands were raised looking for help and, even when help was available, the support staff assumed that trainees knew more than they actually did and, as a result, there was no feeling that a lesson had been learned once the call was over. This led to feelings of nervousness and trepidation within the group as they began to dread the next call as there was at least a small chance that they would have to go over the exact same thing with support staff who were becoming increasingly irritated with being asked the same questions time after time by the same trainee.

2. **Systems training was insufficient:** The group felt that the emphasis on the proprietary computer-based systems was not sufficient as, when agents were live, they may be asked to navigate as many as eight separate screens depending on the nature of the call. Too little time was given over to this during induction while almost no time was allocated for practice. This was partly due to the fact that it took more than three weeks to generate all appropriate system logins for new staff and we had insufficient numbers of working training logins. Most of the systems training was delivered by Powerpoint meaning that hands-on rehearsal was limited to an

hour on the final Friday before moving to Nursery/Grad Bay – clearly not the best preparation for taking your first live calls the following Monday.

3. **Too Few Actual Call Recordings Were Included:** Staff reported that fewer that 10 calls were played to the new trainee groups during their three weeks of induction. They also felt that these calls were deliberately selected to give the impression that the vast majority of interactions with customers would be pleasant and not particularly challenging. This, they believed, was a false impression and did not prepare those about to go live for the 'onslaught' of difficult complaints and rude people they would actually encounter once doing the job 'for real'. All were of the opinion that new staff should be exposed to a larger number of the most difficult call types and customers and that everyone should be trained on how to handle even the most unhappy and demanding callers. The guys who commented claimed that 'hiding' the actual nature of the average call type and customer was making it more likely that a new trainee would leave the business early rather than being 100% honest from day one of the recruitment process regarding what they would have to cope with when going live. General consensus was that no-one really expected every call to be 'a walk in the park' and were happy to go with the flow as long as everyone was trained on how to deal with the worst of customer service situations.

4. **Buddying With Experienced Staff Was Off-Putting:** Each Thursday of the third week of the course our trainers would 'buddy' trainees with experienced call-handlers on the live floor to help them understand what a day of handling calls would

actually feel like. The intention was do help the trainees put their classroom learning into some kind of perspective and support the creation of an individual approach to using the call script in the most bespoke and personalised way. Sadly, the groups I spoke to were of the opinion that this was the day that many considered leaving the business rather than affirming they were ready to make a successful start on a new career in customer service. I heard a lot of complaints about the standard of call-handling they heard whilst listening in to experienced people and the general feeling was that those they had buddied with were unhappy in their jobs and with the company as a whole. Some trainees were actually told to leave as soon as they can as working with us was a totally miserable affair which could end up damaging your mental health!! This feedback was particularly worrying as I'd come across this kind of experience with previous employers and had worked hard with our current L and D people, together with the Team Manager group, to ensure that only highly motivated, enthusiastic staff were selected as buddies for new people and that they should receive training in what would be expected of them should they agree to perform the role. In short, no-one should came away from a buddying experience feeling in any way disillusioned never mind having second thoughts about whether they should remain with the business or not.

5. **Trainers Lacked Energy and Enthusiasm:** It was felt that some of our induction trainers appeared to be less than enthusiastic about both the role of customer service agents and the nature of our key clients. They often expressed concerns about the

nature of the IT systems we were using and the standard of Team Manager trainees would be reporting to. The guys I met with felt that, with the benefit of hindsight, some training staff had insufficient experience of the products and systems they were training on and couldn't deliver the necessary insight into what the job felt like and how to do it to the best of a trainee's ability.

6. **Re-visit Training After Grad Bay:** A sensible, but expensive, suggestion was that all trainees would go back into induction training for two days to allow trainees to discuss their individual experiences and also to allow the training team to go over parts of the role that trainees had found difficult and to cover off call types or systems use that the new guys had found challenging when going live for the first time. As our client only paid us for three weeks of induction training we would have to bear the cost of an extra two days training ourselves or deliver a case to the client that would help them see that paying us for a further couple of days induction would pay dividends in the long run…a hard sell frankly.

Next I asked them about the Nursery or Grad Bay experience. Did they feel it was useful and helpful and what would they change to improve the function? Only one point was made but was made forcefully.

1. **Grad Bay Staff Became Unsupportive After A short Time:** We had selected Grad Bay managers and support staff very carefully. They were all people who had demonstrated the necessary levels of emotional intelligence, expertise and ambition to convince us that they were the right team to get our newest and least experience people from raw trainees to capable

new team members ready to handle most calls effectively in the space of a week. We gave them a half-day of training in how best to support new people then relied on their general 'people skills' to get them through. Unfortunately, most experienced CSAs believed that Grad Bay support staff began the week quickly offering help and support then the newbies needed it but by day three they had started to hide from the raised hands of people looking for help and became impatient and intolerant when having to repeat themselves to trainees who hadn't picked things up the first time. By the end of the week, it was reported, some support staff were completely ignoring raised hands and simply sat in a group talking amongst themselves or sitting at a PC messing about on the internet with little or no supervision from a Team Manager who was there to ensure all new staff were getting the support they required. I had guessed that this was possibly true of one or two of the Grad Bay support staff who we'd taken a bit of a chance on using in that function as an attempt to encourage them to experience a different role within the business and preventing them from becoming bored but I was very disappointed to learn that the accusations of laziness and disinterest could be levelled at the majority of them including the two managers we had used to lead the team. This was very clearly and area we would have to look at urgently if the required improvement in staff attrition numbers was to be achieved. Many of those who volunteered for the support roles believed that this could be a stepping-stone towards a job within the Training team or as a way of getting them noticed ahead of selection for the Team Manager Training

Academy we ran to support the development of the next tranche of operational managers the business would soon require to support our planned growth. The negative feedback received made us question how we had selected and managed the Grad Bay support people but also whether we had a tight enough grip on who the best people might be to take us into the next stage of the overall increase in operational activity we had been expecting.

Naturally there are at least two sides to every story so we recognised that we should take time to ask our existing recruiters, trainers, managers and HR people to express their views on existing processes, trainees and ideas for improving how we should do things in the future. I preferred to run these sessions myself and had considered getting everyone into one big room for a morning and allowing them to express their feelings as a single unit. I was quickly warned off this by a couple of insightful department heads as they had identified that each of the business areas we would be canvassing may prefer to have the opportunity to criticize other business functions and some of the staff within each department. I'm glad I heeded that advice as it soon became clear that there was a great deal of low-level, hidden, bad feeling between Recruitment, Training, Human Resources and Operations and each department relished the chance to freely verbalise their concerns. What follows is a department by department breakdown of the induction related issues staff had identified across the previous couple of years. I've left out the very personal stuff that was clearly designed to colour my view of some apparently disliked members of staff and I've generalised where things got a little too unnecessarily specific around personalities and attitudes. However, it quickly became clear that our current process was perceived as disjointed, fragmented and not trusted as the best way forward in finding the best new people to take our business forward. I had expected a little of the vitriolic feedback from some areas of the business but perhaps not to the extent I actually received it. I can assure you, neither me nor many of my fellow senior managers, were exempt from criticism and the whole thing was a bit of an eye opener that I'm not sure I've fully recovered from!!

Chapter 4

So, let's look at what I was told by the Recruitment team and my first of these meetings. Bear in mind that these are the guys responsible for advertising the roles, collating notes of interest from prospective employees, effecting primary telephone interviews, inviting successful candidates to a face-to-face interview and assessment and, from there, selecting the people who would go on to join us and begin induction training. They would also be responsible for ensuring that all applicants fully understood the nature of the role, what would be expected of them and to give a very clear view of salary, benefits and (very importantly) required commitments to shift patterns. Finally, it was their job to ensure that all new trainees supplied us with the information and paperwork we are required to capture ahead of starting anyone as a salaried employee of the business. References, tax and NI data, proof of address and residency, work related visas, bank details etc. were all fundamental to allowing a new employee to join us on the agreed start date. Many of these things are in fact deal-breakers in terms of us legally employing an individual. Getting it wrong could cost us thousands of pounds in fines and a great deal in the way of reputational damage so we simply had to draw a line and make it very clear that no-one would join us as a member of staff until absolutely everything was in place. Recruiters were provided with a checklist of everything required and admin support to free them up to spend as much time as possible on the job of actually finding and recruiting new staff.

I have to be totally honest at this point and admit that I had been unaware of how much of a challenge it was for our Recruitment Team to bring everything together for each individual at the right time. I was naïve in thinking that anyone keen to work for us would bend over backwards in their efforts to provide us with all the paperwork we required. It seems that almost everyone we employed had at least a few things missing and showed no urgency in getting everything together for us by the required cutoff date.

The first issue they raised was how short the lead time was between receiving the new staff requisition form and having to deliver 15 good quality trainees fully ready to start induction with all the necessary paperwork in place. Time after time, they claimed, we would drop a requirement for anything up to 90 new staff on them and expect them to go out and find us 200-300 decently skilled people to interview ahead of appointing. Often, they said, we would give them as little as four weeks to complete the task. In fact, having checked the previous year's requisitions, the actual average lead time was 6-8 weeks rather than the four they claimed. However, I still had sympathy with how difficult we were making the task for them and made a mental note to investigate how we could change this for the better with immediate effect.

As an outsourced contact centre we would often be asked by clients to ramp up our numbers at very short notice and we prided ourselves on how quickly we could turn things around for the people we worked for. I know the Heads of Recruitment and HR understood that this ability to do things quickly was perceived as a valuable selling point so were 100% committed to supporting operational requirements – even at very short notice. It must be said, however, that they were beginning to identify much lower application and enquiry rates and were becoming convinced that we may have 'saturated' the local area in terms of our total recruitment requirements. Two years previously we could expect to receive up to 50 enquiries for every new intake of 15 FTE but recently that had come down to something closer to 25-30. Also, trying to recruit large numbers of new agents within a short period of time was becoming all but impossible. In the past, finding 100 new people in 8 weeks could be achieved but times had changed. Their experience told them that finding 50 heads over a period of two months would be a major challenge – especially if we wanted to maintain quality standards and keep 90 day attrition rates as low as possible. It would be easy enough to fill requisitions with the right amount of heads but there was every chance that you might lose as much of 25% of the group within the first few weeks. So, in short, they wanted much more time to recruit the required numbers and, ideally, would build a 'bank' of keen, capable people who would be ready to join us as soon as the new staffing requirements were published. They were aware that we had tried this method of recruitment in the past but it had failed as we lost the best members of the bank to competitors who had more immediate requirements for their services than we had. How you keep banked prospective employees enthusiastic about joining us and in a position to refuse any offers from other employers that came their way was destined to be a challenge but one that I was determined to crack. Our Recruitment and HR teams deserved to have the have the best opportunities available to them to find both the numbers and quality of people we demanded of them.

A word of warning on this one; I'll explain later what we put in place to support the recruitment bank project and give details of the kinds of results we achieved. However, unless your business has a couple of unique selling points you will struggle to maintain a list of good people who you can get to join you at very short notice having sat on their hands just waiting for us to get in touch with a start date. Anyone with skills and ambition would simply take the first competitive offer made to them from any employer rather than wait an unspecified amount of time for us to come calling.

Next, our Recruitment colleagues wanted senior management to understand the extent to which finding new people had become more difficult since lockdown rather than easier. Some within the leadership group believed that the offer of hybrid roles where agents could work from home when it best suited them and the business – as well as compulsory time in the main office – meant that people would be queuing to join us as we offered a level of flexibility very different to the ground rules that applied before the pandemic. We generally hoped this would be pretty unique in the local area and would be enough to attract more, rather than fewer, new applicants.

In support of this our Recruitment Manager provided us with a 6 page report and accompanying Powerpoint® presentation breaking down the comparative numbers and highlighting that the same recruitment effort made post lockdown delivered roughly 60% of the number of interested parties when compared to the two years leading up to 2021. Needless to say, the amount of 'quality' applicants reduced in equal proportions meaning that the old methodology just wasn't cutting the mustard in respect of driving the desired high standard headcount as we moved towards the middle of the 2020s. Our partners in both HR and Recruitment were very determined that we should understand the state of the current market and make the necessary adjustments in either our expectations or extent of efforts required to guarantee successful employee resourcing. In short, they wanted us to grow up and realise that the jobs market had changed and that we, as a business, would have to change accordingly.

I'll be honest with you – this one was a bit of a wake-up call for me. I had lost sight of the fact that most people do not really want to work as a call centre agent. Being force fed 35 calls a day – half of which could be from frustrated, angry and downright rude customers – has never been anyone's idea of the start of a great career. We must never ignore the facts on this. These jobs can make people ill. Quality of mental health suffers due to advisers never really being in control of what happens next. This is all against a background of them being subjected to a myriad of automated surveillance and reporting designed to give managers a prompt to intervene and drive consistent and persistent improvement in both behaviours and knowledge. Shove on top of this the constant monitoring of calls for quality purposes and, assuming you possess an ounce of humanity, you can very easily see why these jobs have very little attraction for the majority of individuals other than relatively unskilled people who desperately need to find any kind of work which pays a little better that the minimum wage. Lockdown gave a very large number of people the opportunity to look again at their work choices and many decided that the uncomfortable, pressurized world of contact centres just wasn't an option for them any more. It was patently clear that our business would have to come up with some ways of offsetting the notion that the job itself was unpleasant and possibly a risk to health...not an easy thing to do when you consider that we can never move away from the core requirement for agents to handle a large number of phone calls, chat requests or social media responses across unsociable shift rotas. Responding to these queries would always be the very heart of the role and we would have to offer up a load of side 'benefits' if we were to persuade people to overcome their fears and give us a try. Again, not an easy thing to do when you are trying to keep costs per customer contact as low as possible. Very much something for us to get our collective head around.

It's worth saying that I lost energy on a number of occasions across this exercise. Time after time good people would raise excellent points each of which represented a challenge to how we currently ran the resourcing part of our business. Occasionally it would simply feel we were doing no more than presenting ourselves with a list of seemingly insurmountable problems based on faults in the process we had either failed to recognise or we had kind of known about but simply didn't have the appetite to put right. It became obvious very quickly that improving our recruitment processes would take masses of work, time and resources and that we would have to be honest about the things that we simply could not change due to commercial or practical reasons. We had advertised throughout the business that we were going through this exercise and a large number of interested, engaged and hopeful staff were waiting to see the outcome. Some had very high expectations and were looking to see massive change leading to fast improvements.

In my weaker moments I felt almost like walking away perhaps telling staff that we had taken on board all of their valuable feedback but recognised that the types of changes required to drive very significant improvement would be both expensive and contrary to fundamental business needs. The outcome would have been effectively to maintain the status quo but add in some tinkering around the edges that would be both cheap and easy to do. I really didn't want to do this as it would represent a personal failure and an admission to staff that we, as a business, were not serious enough about living by our 'improvement culture' message we often rammed down people's throats. Frankly, I didn't want to look foolish or give the naysayers the opportunity and ammunition to injure overall morale and characterise the senior management team as toothless, ineffective and (dare I say it) incapable. Go down that route and we make everyone's job more difficult and increase the chance of losing good quality disillusioned staff.

Anyway, the Recruitment guys hadn't finished with their observations and requirements. One major issue for them was the sheer volume of telephone interviews that had to be completed when we gave them a requisition for large numbers of new staff within a short period. Their view was that we should use Operations staff to complete the telephone screening leaving them free to do all the face-to-face stuff and administration that followed offering a new recruit their first role within the business. I would have to think long and hard about this. If I gave Operations Team Managers the instruction to recommend for second interview only those they would be happy to have in their own teams we may end up in a situation where only the very best would be selected whilst the often successful middling group would be rejected as too much of a risk. We would have no chance of driving the kinds of numbers we required. However, if we lowered the bar TMs would be only too happy to tell us at a later date that anyone who was not a success in the role should not have been recruited in the first place and wouldn't have been had we not lowered that particular bar. A bit of a lose/lose situation to be frank.

Across the business we encouraged all staff to find out about other roles and departments and to express an interest in 'shadowing' as part of their annual development plans. Our Recruitment team very much saw this as an opportunity to train up people in other parts of the business to do all of the required recruitment administration that bringing in new people entails. I could see a little sense in this and we quickly asked staff across the floor to volunteer for this training if they had sufficient interest. It did kind of beg the question however of what were the Recruitment team planning to do while the TMs were doing all of the screening interviews and volunteer agents completed all of the required administration? When I asked them this the department manager claimed that his staff should move to supervisory roles overseeing the work of others rather than doing the work themselves. I asked her to go away and think about this as each of her team had been brought into the company on the basis that they were effective, successful, hands-on recruiters. We didn't need supervisors nor all the heartache that would inevitably materialise about increased salaries and changes in contract terms and conditions. I wanted our recruiters to recruit…but recruit a bit more effectively than they had been doing.

In short, the Recruitment team wanted to drop all of the time-consuming drudgery at someone else's door while they devised new middle-management positions for themselves. Needless to say I lost a little respect for them when they came forward with this stuff. There was no admission that they could have done a better job in the past and they were determined to create an easier, unrealistic future for themselves. The idea of accountability just didn't cross their minds. Everyone else was to blame. Poor advertising, short lead times, trainers and operational managers who simply weren't concerned about doing a good job and were only too happy to blame Recruitment for the paucity of the situation. I'm afraid to say they failed to see the irony of their remarks.

Chapter 5

So, where exactly did the Training and Development team believe the issues lay? Who was to blame for previous inadequacies and how could improvements be made. Have a guess!

In my experience trainers have always been a funny (odd) bunch. They often see themselves as a special and separate function within a contact centre. Some see themselves as much as performers as educators and believe themselves to have have a very crucial role in overall business performance. While I don't deny this for a second I have to say I've had a few too many run-ins over the years with training teams and their managers and directors. This may say as much about me as it does them but I have too frequently found them unrealistic and unreasonable to deal with…I must try to improve my approach with these guys!!

Anyway, their first point to me was that the quality of new staff being recruited was much lower than they felt the business required and that too many recruits were simply not capable of being trained to the standard that both our business and our clients expected. They cited lots of examples of people who simply didn't have the level of PC experience required to navigate between screens on our proprietary systems or who were short of the basic communication skills necessary to deal with challenging callers who often had complex queries and possibly unrealistic expectations of very high levels of customer service. In short, they believed that our Recruitment team were delivering excessive numbers of relatively incapable trainees who could not be trained to required standards in the three weeks available to the development guys.

Needless to say, our Head of Recruitment countered this by claiming that his group were under the impression that trainers were lazy and simply wanted top-notch, 'oven-ready' newbies delivered to them on a plate making their jobs as educators easy. He further commented that putting together multiple induction classes of fifteen heads at extremely short notice within a low-paid outsourcing environment meant that the quality of an average new recruit would be much lower than an environment where a hiring organisation took time to select the best of available people from a pool that we simply could not access as an edge-of-town outsourced provider where the local opinion was that we were perceived as a bit of a 'hire and fire', throw stuff at the wall and see what sticks type of employer; a place where only the most unskilled and inexperienced townspeople would expect to have a chance of being employed. I know that's an overly long sentence but I've included it for a reason. I need to reiterate to you that starting this kind of exercise will lead to 'unpleasantness' between different functions within your business. You will be giving them licence to criticize each other with an openness that you won't have experienced other than during after work drinks in a local bar or pub on a Friday evening. A whole load of underlying but unspoken grievance, bias and distrust will immediately spring to the surface and can cause genuine inter-departmental tensions if not managed correctly. There will be times when you'll wish you hadn't even started on your improvement plan.

Our trainers felt that, on average, only five people from each induction group of fifteen were truly fit to be recruited as deliverers of high standard customer service. Only five inductees were fit to absorb and communicate effectively the information held in the system and could quickly and accurately navigate from one screen to another. Most of the other ten in each group would never be able to understand the nature of what the data was telling them or would never achieve the level of basic PC skills required to get from place to place quickly. L and D managers were up against it they claimed. How could they produce fully effective trainees if most weren't in the right capability bracket to achieve what we all wanted? That is, of course, a really good question...assuming they were right about the standard of new recruits being delivered to them by Recruitment. They believed they were being held accountable for failures over which they had no control. To put it simply, if we could give them fifteen trainees with potential then they believed they could spit out fifteen 'finished articles' ready for Grad Bay. I knew we would rarely be able to achieve this so expectations definitely had to be managed going forward both at senior management and at Recruitment and Training levels.

Their next gripe was the standard and format of training materials. Some trainers had visited our clients' home turf and discovered more sophisticated training methods paired with better quality materials which, our trainers believed, supported production lines of better trained, more capable staff. In order to keep our induction courses as inexpensive as possible we had resorted to the traditional classroom model where a trainer talked at fifteen people in a classroom environment for three weeks then released them into the wild on Grad Bay once each trainee had completed a final assessment proving that they take absorbed at least some of the knowledge required to do the job well. Of course we would introduce 'buddying' days where each trainee would pair with an experienced member of staff to listen into calls, observe actions taken and generally discuss the role and its challenges before heading back into the training room for a group discussion around what had been observed. We also had listening sessions when recorded example calls would be played to the group and they would debate the right and wrong ways to proceed based on their training so far. Role play sessions designed to underline the fundamentals of call handling and system navigation would take place throughout the three weeks of induction.

For all my relative distrust of Training departments I did – and still do – have a great deal of sympathy on the subject of the format induction classes tend to take. Let's face it, if the unskilled people we recruit as trainees had been successful in a classroom environment they would have done well at school and college and would not ne working for minimum wage in an outsourced contact centre. Why then, when armed with that knowledge, do we force them into another predominantly classroom based course and expect them to come out the other end expert in their field? We do it because it's cheap and easy to organise. We do not, however, tend to take into account the fact that everyone learns best in their own individual way. Some people have to see things being done before they can have a go themselves, some have to listen and copy speech patterns and vocabulary etc. You'll know that the four main learning styles are Auditory, visual, Kinaesthetic and Read/Write...I know that and so do the people who run my business but not enough is ever done to incorporate each of these teaching methodologies into our induction and on-going training courses. Of course I know why; training redesign is expensive and time-consuming but wouldn't this work pay for itself if it reduced our staff attrition numbers by, say, 10%?

As an industry we must become more aware of how we can support new and existing staff in both learning their roles and also becoming capable and more rounded employees. This means we must consider everything that technology is making available to us to improve in all the areas we operate. If exclusively classroom-based training is 'so last century' we really must look closely at all of the developing alternatives. AI, or machine learning, have become buzz words amongst many people who don't really understand the concept and what it could mean for every aspect of our business. It's going to take a bunch of very forward-thinking marketeers to demonstrate the benefits to the people who own and run contact centres to get us all moving on this. Most people working in our industry simply don't understand the possibilities and implications of introducing hardware and software that mimics the way we, as humans, learn and applies that 'thinking' to every aspect of our existence millions of times a second. In the short term, most simple admin, chat and voice tasks and enquiries will be able to be handled automatically and without human intervention other that some light supervision. In the long term, once the simple stuff has been taken care of, what will the machines learn from what they've already solved and how will they apply it to more complex issues? Will momentum take us into an almost totally automated customer service environment or will AI hit such intransigent brick walls that progress slows to a trickle and we remain in more or less the status quo we see today? I don't know…a little of both probably. The best of us will quickly identify the genuine opportunities for improvement while avoiding the pitfalls of risks to security and increased customer dissatisfaction. In the meantime, it makes sense to look at all available opportunities to improve our induction process and acknowledge that a mixed media approach to training will, in all probability, lead to better outcomes in terms of better prepared staff and fewer leavers.

Finally (I thought), their big gripe was that new trainees simply didn't have sufficient basic PC skills that would allow them to navigate through the numerous systems and screens sufficiently quickly and accurately to deliver effective customer service. The general consensus was that most could struggle through some fundamental internet queries and shove together a rudimentary email but, when push came to shove, the ability to open and work with numerous screens using complex f-key functions while absorbing multiple pieces of information just was not there. The main reason for this is that an individual would have had to have operated in a similar computerised environment for a significant period time in the recent past to be able to have the transferable skills required to adapt quickly to our levels and standards of system use. The majority of new staff had to take the time required to open each relevant screen, note down the required data then move onto another screen and repeat a similar process before compiling a convincing response for the customer based on all the information they had pulled from their trawling of our databases. This meant that a call targeted to last six minutes was actually taking almost double that time or even longer and the quality of information being delivered by our people was usually incomplete and inaccurate leading to repeat calls which, depending on the contracted charging model, would cost either our clients or ourselves hard cash. We simply had to find a way of getting new candidates up to speed before they began customer service training if they were to succeed in the roles and enjoy the job to the extent that they would remain with us for a decent period of time.

My goodness, trainers love to moan and groan don't they? Frankly the people I dealt with had issues with almost every aspect of the recruitment process and, it seemed, Recruitment, HR and Ops Management were all to blame...our clients got it in the neck as well but to a somewhat lesser extent.

As I've mentioned, we liked to try to get new trainees onto the call floor as early as possible to help them understand the nature of the calls or chats they would have to deal with when induction was completed. To ensure this was a positive experience we asked Operations Management to select a number of 'buddies' who would show the new guys the ropes. They would be hand-picked and we could be assured that they would demonstrate all the best possible behaviours when dealing with our newbies. We were all happy with the list of names provided but, in reality, it was very rare that all of the named buddies were available on the call floor at the same time. Shift patterns, planned leave and unplanned time off all seemed to get in the way of this for some reason. Why we couldn't work with our Resource Planning department to ensure that buddying happened at times when most of our named people were on shift I don't know. Trainers also seemed to be a little haphazard in determining when buddying would take place meaning that we could never be assured that the best agents would be available when the new people were paraded onto the floor and forced to sit with experienced team members with a view to picking up some hints and tips.

It seemed pretty straightforward to me that Ops should provide Training and Planning with the names of thirty good agents who, after a certain amount of discussion around what was required of them, were happy to act as positive role models for our inductees. The three departments would then work together well in advance of new courses kicking off to make certain that everyone knew when the buddying exercises would take place and that at least fifteen of our named buddies would be on shift to offer support. This didn't happen and we often ended up with new people listening in to disgruntled or burned out existing staff who would often do everything within their power to try to derail our recruitment by offering trainees the worst possible view of the every day working experience within our organisation. This was their chance to 'retaliate' for any perceived slight or let-down they'd suffered during their time with us and my goodness many of them snapped up the opportunity. All too often, trainees came off the floor feeling unhappy and demotivated due to negativity from existing staff who should never have been selected as buddies in the first place but were forced into that position due to a complete lack of planning. Worryingly, Ops Management told us that they often couldn't find enough willing, positive call-handlers to act as buddies and never really got their heads around that the lack of good, strong role models was in part due to their inability to manage staff in the way that they always hoped they would be managed i.e. with consideration, humanity, flexibility and emotional intelligence or insight. Clearly, this was going to be a massive piece of work in its own right but, it's worth saying, these levels of dissatisfaction were not apparent in the annual employee engagement survey.

So, the trainers believed that Ops staff were responsible for draining new trainees of their enthusiasm and optimism by filling their heads with notions of inflexibility around shifts and planned leave, incompetent managers, poor technology and on-going payroll issues during buddying. They also felt that agents exaggerated the hassle of the day-to-day role in that they claimed the proportion of rude and difficult customers was far higher than had been described during both the recruitment and induction process and that the job was dehumanising and demoralising with no obvious route of escalation to a manager when requested by a particularly difficult customer leading to complaints about process and staff who could not have done anything differently.

Learning and Development also believed that a change in how we distributed training time across the initial three weeks was essential. Rather then three full weeks of induction followed by release into an Operations related Grad Bay environment it was felt that trainees should be allocated Grad Bay in the second day of week three then, at the end of days three, four and five of that last week trainees should return to training classes to discuss and revise the key areas of learning they feel they will need expertise in when they go live. This would be based on the types of calls they had handled during Grad Bay and the gaps in their knowledge they identified across each day. The experienced Ops Grad Bay support staff could also feed into these sessions to help trainers understand where they should be concentrating their revision. I have a lot of sympathy with this approach but it can be really difficult to adjust induction training timetables when they have been planned by our clients and when there's a great deal of information to squeeze into the existing three week period. It doesn't mean it can't be done – reduce the number of buddying sessions for example – so definitely worth considering.

Finally, at last, our Training managers made it abundantly clear that they didn't believe that we had the right people working with new staff in our nursery/Grad Bay. They were concerned that we had utilised Operations-minded people who had ambitions to be managers rather that those with the correct levels of knowledge and emotional intellect needed to nurture new staff into competency and confidence. From feedback received from ex-trainees they felt that Grad Bay support had historically been impatient, disparaging and disrespectful. They simply didn't have the kind of tolerance required to answer the same questions time after time in a helpful and informative way. In fact, Training told us, if we genuinely wanted to get to the heart of why so many new staff left the business soon after induction was complete then we should look no further than Grad Bay support and the transition from there to live Operations teams. In essence their contention was that Operations senior agents and Team Managers made some people feel so uncomfortable that they felt that staying with our business in an agent role was simply going to be too uncomfortable and distressing and, frankly, long shifts in a local burger drive-through would actually be a more pleasant and worthwhile experience.

Naturally, as a Senior Operations Manager, I took all of this with a very large pinch of salt. I knew all of the people involved in Grad Bay support well and had given my approval in the form of sign-off to allow them to take on these temporary roles. In many cases the support guys weren't too long out of induction themselves and had shown all the necessary attributes required to make me feel comfortable that they were ideally suited to helping our trainees reach competency quickly and effectively. In addition, I trusted 100% the management team we had asked to run nursery – they were amongst our most considerate and empathetic managers and had been hand-picked to run the show. Could I really have got this so wrong? I guess I'd have to have an open mind but, given my pretty entrenched view of Training departments, that was going to be difficult.

Anyway, we're getting very close to the point where I can tell you what we did about all of the perceived issues that had been identified across the business and, most importantly, what worked and what didn't.

But first, a very brief chapter on what the Operations people felt could be done to improve our recruitment, on-boarding, training and nursery processes. What did they believe we could do to give them the best opportunity of integrating highly capable people into their existing Ops teams?

Chapter Six

You're not going to be too surprised at what the Operations teams told us about where they felt the inadequacies lay in respect of each aspect of our recruitment and training processes. There was no love lost between them and most other functions within the business so they weren't going to be slow to tell us how they actually felt. They gave us it with both barrels so to speak while, at this point in the process at least, we did not retaliate with the negative feedback on Operations received from Recruitment, HR, L and D, Planning, IT et al. Again, everyone was to blame apart from them.

Let's start with how they felt about the job being done by our Recruitment people. While there was a certain empathy towards the team in that we all realised how difficult it could be for them to find large numbers of good quality with very little notice, the Ops guys believed that far too many people were joining us who simply didn't have the correct fundamentals in place to allow them to flourish in what they believed was a pretty challenging environment and complex role.

Managers in Grad Bay and, subsequently after new agents had gone live, quickly sensed that 'at least half' of all new trainees either didn't have sufficient PC experience or lacked the required customer service and communications skills to be effective in the role. They felt that the best of the poor performers could possibly make the grade with sufficient coaching support but the remainder were something of a hopeless cause and would be better off working in other environments where these skills were less essential. In particular, those who had insufficient IT skills would require weeks and weeks of specialist training to get them to the required standard. Far too many newbies couldn't even understand the most basic functions required to make a decent fist of the roles they had been employed for. Especially worrying was the lack of understanding of the principles required to become an effective chat focussed agent meaning that navigation through proprietary systems screens could not be accessed quickly and accurately and the standard of written English was deemed so poor that some new starts were passed off as only semi-literate. Team Managers believed that they simply would not have the time and resources required to get these people up to speed and that a lack of secondary school education was at the heart of why these guys in particular weren't fit to commit to the role. Managers were not school teachers I was told time and time again and didn't have the skills required to take the poorer inductees from semi-literate to literate within a reasonable time period.

Operations Managers insisted that our Recruitment team should take much more time to test applicants' PC skills and also their ability to communicate in writing in simple accurate English. A basic minimum standard threshold should be established for both and, anyone failing to reach this standard, should not be considered for employment.

If an exercise such as this is to succeed in the long-term a number of things have to happen and a whole bunch of people must stay on board right till the end. Incremental and prolonged success will be dependent on senior sponsors remaining enthusiastic while the drones put the key elements of the programme in place day after day until the new practices are embedded. It will take levels of focus and determination that you may not have had to insist on before in your career. Believe you me this will not be easy.

We lost the backing of key directors and heads of department on a number of occasions across the length of our project. Many felt that the bad feeling being generated between functions was potentially too damaging and that the benefits of the upside did not outweigh the the detriment being caused elsewhere in the business. In fact, one or two very senior people began to believe that poor recruitment and high levels of staff turnover should simply be regarded as necessary costs of doing business and we should build these into our financials from day one. They felt that we were throwing the baby out with the bathwater and possibly destroying levels of trust and morale that had taken years to build.

This was particularly disappointing as the two directors involved had been amongst the keenest proponents of change when we kicked off some weeks before.

Should you decide to implement a programme of extensive change within your organisation I really must insist that you understand that no such change can happen without peoples' noses being put out of joint and animosity will raise its very ugly head time and time again. Do not expect a free run without meeting significant challenge from people you may like and respect. No-one sits happily in the background saying nothing while a team of busybodies rips apart the attitudes and processes that bosses and their teams have taken years to develop and evolve. You will lose friends and it's crucial that you understand this and take steps to minimise the damage from the get-go and also plough through later in the project when things will inevitably get tough. You must learn the arts of moderation, diplomacy and compromise at the earliest possible stage and, indeed, when you introduce the notion of your change programme – right back at the very start – you have to tell every senior person in the business that they must expect high levels of discontent to bubble up within their teams and that they must do everything within their powers to prevent relationships being damaged irreparably. This won't stop the bad stuff happening but will take some of the sharpest edges off the worst parts. It also gives directors and their senior managers to weigh up whether they really want this exercise to go ahead or should the business look at a less intrusive approach where small, almost gentle change is implemented and no existing staff members have to feel persecuted.

Anyway, after that preamble, let's get to the heart of things: what did we do with the feedback? How did we implement next steps? What were the outcomes...was any of it worth doing? What do I suggest you do in similar circumstances?

As I mentioned at the outset, we had agreed in advance that each distinct business area or function would agree to move forward on three separate goals. One action would be something that could be done almost immediately, another that could be successfully completed within 3-6 months and finally something more ambitious that could be in place after a period of 12 months. We would use a loose form of Pareto Analysis to determine what we would each focus on.

Essentially this means we would take an 80:20 approach to decide where we should aim our focus – i.e. identify the 20% of actions that would impact of 80% of your most prominent issues or obvious areas for development which may have become neglected or been ignored up until this point. As our American CEO put it at the time, it was crucial that we didn't try to 'boil the ocean' at this juncture. In his view we should make small to medium sized changes and get them right rather than be overly ambitious, try to achieve too much then effectively fail due to becoming overwhelmed. We had to realise that 98% of our focus had to remain on running the existing business as well as we could while beavering away continuously in the background on a small handful of recruitment and retention related ambitions and not take our collective eye off the ball in attempting to solve issues that, while important, were not business-critical at that juncture. This made a lot of sense at the time and still does. There is no point in getting carried away with change just for the sake of it. If your business is stable and profitable then change, although essential if your organisation is to move forward, cannot become your raison d'aitre. Driving the highest of day-on-day standards while maintaining strong performance and staff satisfaction has to be the reason you go to work. Unless your business is in a total mess change management should always remain a sub-industry for senior management: something good and essential but not anyone's reason to get up in the morning.

As planned we put in place a change team headed up by an experienced project manager who would keep us all honest and on track even when something else shiny came along and distracted us from our previous good intentions. I'm not exaggerating when I say that the appointment of this individual could be the difference between a successful improvement plan and a total failure. Without the change programme being driven by a competent and sensitive individual all of the organisations original good intentions will dissipate, diminish and – eventually – disappear. Why? Well, because real life gets in the way. Things will happen that put plans for change on the back burner.

Governance of all this stuff is so important. It kind of goes without saying that all relevant parties should know the part they are playing and what their obligations to the group are. They should also understand what everyone else is up to and what the intended outputs are. Regular group and sub-group meetings should take place where minutes are taken and actions should follow. The format of all documentation should be professional and consistent (there are loads of templates on the internet if you're looking for a shortcut on this).

We decided that a weekly meeting of heads of departments should take place followed by a brief update to our sponsors within the business. Often there wouldn't be too much to report so it was really just a case of the project manager and perhaps two heads of department sitting with the HR Director and covering off where we were against project/programme plan and listing any highlights or lowlights with a view of next steps. As the project progressed these meetings were often cancelled and, after about three months, we agreed that they should happen every two weeks or even monthly if there wasn't much to tell people.

It is also crucially important to report back on progress to each function within the business which had contributed all of the important the feedback and data we initially required to kick the whole thing off. Needless to say each of these departments had actions of their own but they also needed to understand what everyone else was up to and how what they were accountable for delivering would feed into the success of the overall campaign. It was massively important to celebrate and small wins as momentum could all too easily be lost during a change project that took more that a year to fully implement and the results of which may not be seen for even longer. We achieved this by ensuring that heads of department held regular feedback sessions with their key people and that a sanitised version of our progress was reported to the whole business through our corporate intranet pages. All members of staff were encouraged to comment and ask questions via the intranet site and we worked hard to respond as honestly as we could to each sensible enquiry. It was very important for all to understand that this would be a long-term project and that the results would not be seen for anything up to two years. As you can imagine, 90% of employees probably didn't picture themselves to be still working within our business in 24 months so what we published wasn't always of interest to everyone and it gave the most disgruntled within the employee community the chance to blow off steam and offer the kinds of observations that were little more than acute criticisms of people, processes or historical incidents with which they had some kind of issue.

Now finally, ahead of getting down to the nitty-gritty of what we actually planned, did, experienced then measured, I have to emphasise the importance of getting the reporting of all activities into a suitably professional format that can be easily digested by staff and management alike. It must be clear and insightful, but most importantly, honest about the success or otherwise of any on-going change programme. No apologies for going so strong on this one as results have to be intelligently measured and there should be no fear around calling out difficulties or, indeed, failures when they arise – as they surely will.

This role has to fall to an area of the business commonly regarded as least impacted by the successes or failures of the campaign and which would widely be regarded as trustworthy by the employee and leadership communities. We asked our HR and Management Information departments to cover this role for us headed by the Director of Human Resources. It became their job to produce a monthly report highlighting key numbers or agreed key performance indicators relating to each of our recruitment and staff retention targets including comparisons to last month's and last year's results in the same agreed areas of focus. They would also produce an executive summary commenting on challenges and successes together with a view on overall progress being made against plan. The HR Director would go through this with the company's board of executives at each monthly general board meeting and take relevant questions. She would then deliver any feedback from these sessions to the project leadership committee as soon as possible after the board meeting.

   Further to this, it was the HR Director's responsibility to inform all staff through the company intranet of how the programme was progressing and to highlight any signs of success. Failures and challenges were not ignored or glossed over in these commentaries but I have to be honest and let you know that we did carefully 'manage' some of the information we delivered to staff through our intranet pages. Our reasons for this were pretty legitimate in my view as numbers or ill-defined comments taken out of context can paint an overly negative picture which, with the potential for people outside our business to be made aware of our numbers, may incorrectly impact on how the general public believed our business was performing. For example, the local newspaper was consistently pressing staff for salacious, less than positive gossip around the inside working of our centre and we didn't want to give the impression that we had excessively high staff turnover or were struggling to recruit in the local area as both of these sentiments could easily be worked up into something that just wasn't the case...i.e. that operating out of this particular location was no longer working for us and that we may have been considering a full or part move to another part of the country. Our intention had always been to publish a press release at a point close to the end of the project celebrating the extent to which, due to intensive recent activity, we were now even more successful when it came to attracting new staff and retaining our extremely happy existing people thus demonstrating that our centre had become an even better place to work. Anything overly negative in the form of monthly intranet insights could have given a totally different perspective on the progress we believed we were making.

So, there we had it. Our light-touch project governance was in place and every relevant individual was clear on the part they were playing. What follows is a breakdown of each agreed objective assumed by each business function together with a summary of the outcomes we observed and a commentary on what worked for us and what didn't. I'll conclude with a few remarks on how I think you should progress should you decide to put together a similar improvement plan and I'll be pretty clear on what I think it best for you to avoid. Having run these projects on three occasions now I think I can be pretty certain around what works and what doesn't; what is essential and what should be avoided.

Chapter 7

As you can see in the chapter that follows, each department (eventually) agreed to take on three goals. The first would represent the low-hanging fruit or something that could be achieved almost immediately through small changes in attitude and process. The second goal should be more challenging and require both effective planning and organisation to support it being achieved. The third objective would require comprehensive organisational change and may need up to 12 months to embed.

Each department decided on their own goals then attempted to persuade the senior management group that each was indeed a worthwhile priority and that they had a strong chance of completing the objective on time and in a way that would have a measurable positive impact on staff recruitment or retention. This wasn't as straightforward as it sounds as there was a little bit of in-fighting amongst individual staff members around what should be regarded as a 'worthwhile' goal and what could be deemed a 'priority'. Even more awkward were the conversations between department heads and senior management groups concerning the actual value to the business of the objectives they had selected. It is fair to say that some department heads felt that others were not being sufficiently ambitious and, in one case, the Head of Recruitment was told that his objectives were simply everyday or business as usual commitments that every other function had expected them to be getting on with anyway. In fact, it was stated that he 'should be embarrassed' to offer up his suggested goals as they really just looked like a list of things that Recruitment a a team wanted the rest of the business to do on their behalf.

I'm afraid I had to agree. Everything coming from Recruitment was angled at criticising the rest of the business for making their lives more difficult and offering nothing to support the 'exhausted' Recruitment team who clearly had been failing for some time.

Frankly, most of our organisation felt that the Recruitment team was lazy and badly led. It felt like every meeting with them ended in frustration at their lack of positivity and that their leader wasn't prepared to attempt anything new or challenging. Our Executive Director group were beginning to feel the same and expressed this view privately to both the Head of Recruitment and Director of HR to whom he reported. Pressure was imposed on them to change their approach and lead the rest of the business on the proposed changes to our recruitment methodology in a way that energised everyone connected with that function. In return, each other area of the business would offer manpower to support them in their request for support in interviewing, administration and technology. That wasn't a problem for me in Operations as I had a number of staff desperate to dip their toes into the world of recruitment and some had aspirations to move full-time to that environment. I could easily find them six good guys to help out when required.

Before we even got started on the new improvement plan our Head of Recruitment resigned and took one of his team with him. Rather than hold us back these changes offered up an opportunity to go and find a new energetic and enthusiastic recruitment professional who would both head up the team and ensure the success of our new plan of action. It allowed us to bypass the proposed unambitious goals put forward by the former recruitment head and impose our own much more strategic and integrated ideas which the new person would pick up simply as a fait accompli and, indeed, the new recruit would be selected on criteria which demonstrated their willingness to put everything they had behind the new objectives. Losing the previous incumbent waws not really an issue. He had run his race and had little more to offer either his team or the business as a whole. He saw himself as a realist and presented himself as 'the voice of reason' at meetings of departmental heads when, in fact, he was actually perceived as overly-negative and tended to suck the energy out of any relevant new proposal. Although we were glad to see the back of him we made sure that his successes were suitably celebrated publicly and gave him a dignified and well-meant send-off. At his leaving night he drunkenly took me aside to let me know that he thought I was pretty hopeless and that I'd be the next senior manager to be forced out of the business. He believed I had let him down by not supporting his negative, ill-thought-out criticisms of how we operated. I told him that I was sorry that he felt that way but couldn't agree with how he presented himself, wished him well in the future then stepped back to watch as he told everyone at his party, individual by individual, how poor he thought they were at their jobs and that they had let him down. Just before midnight he was man-handled against his will into a taxi by two of his team who were becoming increasingly concerned for his safety and that was the last any of us saw of him. A thoroughly undignified ending to a two-year career with us that started with so much promise but ended in ignominy because an individual who had all the required skills simply ran out of steam, became complacent and lazy and totally lost his ability to consider and drive positive change. If he had continued in the role as he had started he could have been director material but, to use football parlance, he 'lost the dressing room' after about 18 months. He couldn't keep the exec team on-side and his own direct reports lost respect for him. His way of dealing with this was to bring all of their moans and groans to meetings of senior staff in an effort to show that he had their backs. All it did was irritate the rest of us and demonstrate that he had lost the respect of his group. He was a decent man who lost his way but blamed everyone else. He couldn't handle drinking alcohol and didn't make the most of the dignified and respectful route out of the business that had been set up for him. Last I heard he was working as a Recruitment Consultant working for a city agency and I sincerely hope he does well and has learned the lessons he experienced while working with us.

We received 17 applications for the vacant role of Head of Recruitment. After much discussion we reduced this to the top three candidates on paper and invited then for a first interview. This would be followed by a more intensive second interview then a rubber stamp follow-up. We wanted all of this to happen very quickly and were keen to appoint as soon as possible so that the successful candidate had time to consider our offer then work their notice in any existing job they had. Our final three was made up of two existing 'Heads of' and someone who had been in a Recruitment Team Manager role for two years and was now looking for their first 'Head of' position. The advantage this person had was that she was working in on outsourced contact centre environment at the time of application and had a very strong understanding of the kinds of challenges faced by our kind of business. She possibly lacked experience when it came to planning strategy and in communications with senior stakeholders at board level but these things can be learned and, assuming decent mentoring, we felt she could learn these skills pretty quickly. The two other candidates were not from a contact centre background but both were extremely polished and professional in how they went about presenting themselves.

I wasn't involved in the interview and selection process other than being part of the panel that selected the final three to go through to the interview stages. I was, however, cheered by the positive feedback from the interview panel about how all three performed at the first interview. Both experienced candidates were slick, corporate and impressive – the young woman was raw but massively enthusiastic, knowledgeable about contact centre recruitment in out local area and, crucially, determined to make our recruitment improvement plan work. Both of the other candidates were keen to support the plan but took the view that they would have to review the strengths of the team they were inheriting and our previous recruitment practices before committing themselves to a new improvement plan as a fait accompli. In normal circumstances this would be entirely understandable but, as a business, we had to begin to see improvement in the very short term if we were to meet our staffing requirements going forwards. We simply didn't have to time to sit around waiting 3-6 months for an individual to tell us if they would be able to support or plans or not. In fact, one of the two experienced guys had three months' notice to work on ending his existing contract so it could have easily been six months before he was in a position to tell us whether he was supporting the plan or not.

We decided to really push all three candidates at second interview on their ability to accept the current improvement plan and make it work for us over a twelve month period. As feared, the two experienced people told us they were unwilling to commit to the new plan as it may prove unrealistic bearing in mind they had no insight into the current state of local recruitment. I was massively disappointed to hear this. We had just lost an individual who appeared to be doing everything he could to make change difficult and there really didn't seem much point in taking a chance on someone who may, albeit very professionally, come back to us and say they were unwilling to fully support our new requirements.

The third candidate was so keen to win her first Head of Recruitment role that we were worried that she would naively agree to almost anything we asked her to achieve in the first 6-12 months of her employment. However, we gave her a chance and I'm really glad we did. Our thinking was that her enthusiasm and determination to drive low-level change would be enough to drive the short-term improvements we had failed to see for some time in what was, frankly, a stagnating part of the organisation. The warmth of her personality would, we hoped, endear her to both her new team and the leaders of the other functions she would be expected to interact with. She also brought new ideas based on what had worked in her previous working environment – something the other two candidates would not be able to do. We did have some initial minor issued around how she presented herself during meetings with senior management but we put this down to being overly keen to be seen to be both contributing and doing well and we were comfortable that her line manager, the Director of HR, could coach her through how best to achieve what she wanted at senior staff meetings without giving the impression that she either wasn't listening to directors or that she knew better that them.

In fact, after one meeting I took her for a coffee and tried to gently help her understand that she could be perceived as a successful professional within the business without constantly talking over experienced senior people or, even worse, publicly diminishing their ideas and observations because she had been through similar less than successful initiatives with her previous employer. In her previous role she had not been exposed to high-level meetings and had been free to speak her mind within the safe environment of her her small junior management team. She had never learned how to present material to senior management or that a director with twenty-five years experienced doesn't enjoy being told that he doesn't really know what he's talking about by a new, more junior member of staff...especially in front of his peer group of exec team members. There were tears when I fed this back but I guess that was out of frustration more than anything else and in the end her boss took on the mantle of educating her on how to get the best results when dealing with senior managers' egos and, most importantly, how to get them on-side and keep them there. She was simply so keen to make quick improvements that she failed to see that she was potentially stepping on some highly influential toes. Anyway, we got there in the end and, most importantly, she drove through the proposed changes to our recruitment model with boundless energy and enthusiasm. She also managed keep her team with her throughout which surprised us as we had begun to believe that some of the recruitment guys had lost there verve and determination to do well in the role. We had planned for at least two leavers given that they had lost the protection of their previous Head of Recruitment. That didn't happen and the whole of the existing group appeared to buy into the proposed changes and the persistent, on-going activity required to make them a success.

So, what were the Recruitment team's three new objectives and how did they go about achieving them?

To decide this we embarked on an 'away day' where our team of executive directors and heads of department took a trip to a local hotel, switched off phones and email and came up with and agreed on three objectives for each of the relevant teams. Our objective was simple – come up with a joined-up approach to improving the results of our agent recruitment process while reducing overall levels of staff attrition (leavers) with particular focus on those leaving the business within 90 days. Target numbers were thrown around the room ranging from the conservative to the impossible. Eventually we agreed on moderate improvement targets that we believed we could build on in year two once we had a clear view of what our initial actions had achieved.

We first looked at what our Recruitment team would want to achieve and at how they would alter their processes to support their ambitions.

Their narrative was pretty simple; they wanted us to be able to offer superior rates of pay and better shift options (including home working opportunities) to help us attract those employed at our local competitors. They also wanted us to develop a 365 days-a-year recruitment strategy meaning they could distribute their efforts across the whole 12 month period rather than in six hectic 'blip' points when clients made short-term demands. They asked that we used specialist help to develop assessments, interviews and questionnaires designed to identify recruits with the 'right' potential and characteristics for success rather than simply the traditional gut feel based attempts that favoured applicants with contact centre or customer service experience. We had done some work around profiling the people who had joined us in the last twelve months and gone on to some success within their roles and across the business as a whole. Surprisingly, over 90% of our best people had little no experience of a similar role but could be identified by other attributes such as long-term membership of organisations like the Scouts or Brownies, persistence over a number of years in other unconnected employment types or devotion to a particular charity, individual or group of individuals who relied on the applicant for support. Age, sex and family status often proved similar – if obvious – indicators of those people most likely to take a new role seriously and who would dedicate themselves to improvement if the business offered the right kind of support to them.

For reasons we couldn't quite fathom, applicants with a lot of relevant experience often proved to be the most unsettled and likely to move on citing irritation with management and processes as their reasons for frustration. I made the point that, if we were keen to improve hourly pay rate and shifts to help attract experienced contact centre people and those considering out competitors, should we not be taking steps to ensure that we were attracting the right kind of people and not simply perpetuating the conveyor belt of dragging experienced people from our rival centre up the road one month then watching them leave with their arms up in disgust 90 days later. Could it be that, by some form of implication during the recruitment process, our new, experienced staff believed they were simply walking in to an environment ripe for them to take up promoted or alternative roles in double-quick time? Perhaps this is why they were leaving in frustration after such a short period of time. It has always been massively important that all new joiners are aware that they are joining an organisation which prides itself on offering all talented and enthusiastic staff a bunch of opportunities to develop and take on new, more complex roles. However, we should be careful not to infer to anyone – irrespective of experience – that they would be promoted to a role of their choice soon after completion of training. Of course, if they apply themselves to their initial tasks in a way that suggests talent then we would be delighted to help them move forward. There could be no question, however, of new experienced people simply walking into promoted roles based solely on what they had done elsewhere. Any such 'deal' would deter inexperienced people from taking a risk with us as they would see themselves as starting the race from behind our recruits who had worked in contact centres in the past.

As mentioned earlier, over the last ten years our younger potential applicants have made it clear that they wanted to work for an employer whose values aligned with their own. They wanted to be associated with a business which was well known for supporting local charities and community organisations and which took a tolerant view of inclusion irrespective of gender, sexuality, creed, religion, colour etc. Our Recruitment colleagues insisted that we should have a really strong story to tell covering each of these key areas. They wanted us to be the best-known business locally for promoting diversity and the benefits of business in the community. Our new Head of Recruitment came to us with a plan to guarantee comprehensive coverage in the local media on a monthly basis of all of our good works throughout the areas where most of our staff lived. We already gave staff one day a year that they could use to support local charities but, to be honest, hadn't put our collective backs into ensuring this drove the kind of social capital and goodwill which would look like good value for money – allowing 800 staff to take a paid day off work could cost as much as £100k per annum so it was terrifically important that it became a worthwhile exercise both in terms of the good the campaign was doing for the community and the PR benefit to the business. It was agreed that we should relaunch our Business in the Community package to staff, local charities and the media based in our immediate environment and that a small team should be made responsible and accountable for planning all events and ensuring that maximum media coverage was achieved. A quarterly meeting with senior executives would keep us informed of what had been achieved and what would be happening next. This group would work with our IT staff to ensure that the company website and the new company dedicated recruitment website would be saturated with news of our good works throughout the area.

So, in summary, what did our new Head of Recruitment want to achieve at the conclusion of this exercise and what goals did she accept on behalf of her team?

She made it very clear that she wanted her group to be recruiting 365 days a year building a pipeline of new recruits who would be selected using new attitude-based criteria rather than solely experience markers. These recruits would be 100% aware of both the benefits of working with us and the challenges of the role – there must be no room for confusion or opportunity for even one single recruit to tell us that they were surprised at the difficult nature of the job and that it simply 'wasn't for them'. We should be able to use a range of advertising channels to attract new staff who would fully comprehend that we were offering the best hourly rate, most flexible, family friendly shift patterns within a community conscious business determined to show the locality how much we cared. There must be no concerns over inclusivity and that anyone with the right attitude could join us and build a worthwhile career in a way that may not be possible elsewhere in our vicinity. A range of unique selling points should be available to the team to use as points of persuasion when competing for new staff. Finally, operations staff should be free to support at pinch points when the administration burden threatened to overload the Recruitment team.

The agreed goals we arrived at were:

Short Term Goal:

Work with Finance and Planning to ensure that our offered hourly rate and range of shifts on offer were actually the best available in comparison to our competitors in the locality then ensure that this message was being delivered to all potential recruits at every available opportunity. Plan monthly recruitment drives – irrespective of immediate staffing requirements – to support the building of a pipeline we could draw on at any point when clients required to ramp up. Develop a regime designed to maintain buy-in from successful new recruits for whom we didn't yet have available training places.

Medium Term Goal:

Work with PR and IT to ensure we had a dedicated recruitment website containing videos of actual staff telling their success stories. Examples of a sceptical under-25 year old who needed to be assured of the community focus of the business, a mum with kids who wasn't sure she could meet the shift requirements and a retired police officer who wasn't at all sure that he would fit in to a totally different working environment to that which he had been used to for the previous 30 years. Videos and blogs should maintain a narrative of how challenging the role could be (especially at the beginning of one's career) but that perseverance could result in fun, security and progress within an extremely professional and rewarding environment.

Long Term Goal:

Build and promote a community focussed ethos and set of easily communicated values we could use to provide content to the local media on, at least, a monthly basis which both reassured the town that this was an organisation that had the wellbeing of local people at the heart of our decision making process and which supported all staff in giving their time and energies to local good causes. A new campaign to encourage existing staff to introduce new recruits to us should be rewarding and something which delivered positivity and success to all three parties rather that previous attempts which ended in embarrassment and complaints about payments not being made where due.

Now, there are some big asks in there. Adding just 10p to the hourly rate of every call/chat handler would cost the business an extra £250k per annum. While deliberately building in planning efficiencies to our staffing to facilitate more user-friendly shift patterns could prove equally expensive as each additional FTE increases costs by approximately £30k each year after building in training and National Insurance. A great deal of work would have to be done around ensuring the part-time/full-time balance was correct and that unfunded overtime as reduced to an absolute minimum. Contact centres have battled with these challenges for almost fifty years without coming up with a universally satisfactory solution so it seemed pretty unlikely that we were going to solve the age old equation as part of this exercise alone.

On the upside, our 90 day leavers' rate was sitting at 40%...that's 6 people out of every new training group of 15 while annual attrition had been as high as 80% - 8 out of 10 newbies would be gone by the end of a 12 month period. With each leaver costing somewhere between £2k and £2.5k it was easy to see the kinds of savings that could be made if we could, say, half the number of leavers in any one year. A rough calculation would drop the cost of staff turnover from an estimated £1.2 million to 'just' £600k...even more if we could get closer to 30% annual attrition. So, a hell of a gamble, but an investment of maybe £350k could drive savings of £600k-£700k and improve our reputational capital enormously. The investment would be spread across a year with very little required up front meaning that it all felt do-able while monthly reviews would tell us if we should be pulling the plug if we reached a point where costs were exceeding savings. Also, we could phase in our improvements. A 5p increase in hourly rate would make us more competitive as we already matched what our local rivals were doing and we needn't jump in with both feet on the scheduling piece as any well-publicised improvement in the family-friendly nature of what we asked employees to do for us may actually be enough to encourage new recruits to select us rather that our competitors and, perhaps, help attract the best of their existing agent communities.

Add to that a massive splurge of publicity highlighting the community-focussed approach our business was now taking towards our relationship with local people along with a number of events which clearly demonstrated the nature of our socially conscious corporate values and we may just find that we would be in a position to attract and retain numbers and types of staff we hadn't previously been able to reach – especially if we were starting to become attractive in ways that our competitors hadn't quite got around to yet. Needless to say, similar local employers would see what we were up to and react accordingly and we would have to be ready for their responses. However, if we got in their first and make a really good job of it we may have stolen a march which could last for up to three years.

Learning and Development (Training)

As usual, Training were an awkward bunch to deal with. The things they wanted to change, for the most part, were actually the responsibility of other parts of the business so we had to 'encourage' them to see their objectives as partnerships with other functions...including some of our biggest and most important clients whose business essentially sustained our organisation as a going concern. As you can imagine, we had to manage the relationships between L and D and our clients extremely carefully since, on a bad day, even our most senior Training staff could go off like a box of fireworks and undermine the good relations we had with our most lucrative customers. We got there in the end but not without quite a lot of heartache and heart to heart conversations with individuals who were a little too keen to disrupt the status quo. In fact we had two remove two trainers from dealing directly with client staff as they were only too keen to explain to client experts where they were going wrong and how they should go about changing the basis of what they had worked on and evolved over years. This became very personal indeed and I took the decision to change key personnel at the first opportunity while giving the impression that 'passion' and inexperience had led our guys to overstep the mark and removed them from client relations while going through some very necessary development. We replaced them with a couple of less innovative but far more level heads and that seemed to do the trick.

In essence, our trainers wanted to totally redesign much of our existing client proprietary induction courses and remove the emphasis from a presentation-focussed, classroom style of approach to something much more hands-on and immersive with Operations picking up almost 50% of the responsibility for getting our newbies into a place good enough that they could handle most call types effectively from day one. They also told the business that we should manage each interaction a trainee had with existing staff by selecting a very large number of operational staff to act as side-by-side coaches, demonstrators and mentors throughout the first four weeks of a new person's employment with us. Finally, they insisted that instead of three weeks training we should devise a new four week course during which trainees would return to the classroom at the end of each day and discuss what they had learned or failed to understand with the best available people from Operations. They couldn't see why Trainers should be involved in that part of the exercises as they – in their own minds – had completed what we had tasked them with i.e. hammering home all the information required to be an effective agent at a basic level.

Now, there's some good stuff in there I'm happy to admit but I wasn't content with L and D reducing their input by 50% and passing the remainder across to Operations. I also had to take time to explain to them the possible cost involved in recruiting, training and managing a very large group of experienced specialist agents who would operate as mentors to each new trainee. A lovely idea in a perfect world but simply not something we could afford to commit to at this point in the growth of the business. Although returning to the classroom at the end of every floor-based training day or nursery activity was universally agreed to be a good idea, the cost of adding a fourth week of induction training would be prohibitive so we had to find a halfway house where we could design this into the induction programme without any extra cost to the business. So, in the end (after an awful lot of discussion) L and D agreed to pick up the following objectives:

Short Term Goal:

Work with Operations to ensure that we have at least 30 heads on each campaign trained to act as side-by-side support mentors when live floor training is required. The best of these should progress to working in Grad Bay and ultimately train as learning co-ordinators or Team Managers. Attitude as well as competence must come as a prerequisite as we no longer wanted to expose new staff to disgruntled and negative employees. Three monthly reviews of all mentors performance including 360 degree feedback should be booked into the diary for the next 12 months.

Work with Resource Planning to ensure that a suitable numbers of mentors would be scheduled in on any shift where live floor training was planned

Medium Term Goal:

Work with Operations to create one hour per day classroom feedback and revision sessions each day in the week of Grad Bay. The purpose would be to allow trainees to tell Training and Operations staff where they were having challenges and for complex topics to be simplified and retrained. These sessions MUST be run bt Training and Ops combined and not solely by Operations as they would be unaware of what had been covered during induction.

Long Term Goal

All areas of the business agreed that induction should be simplified to focus on the five main call or query types which represented approximately 80% of all calls received. A concerted move away from presentation/classroom style training methods to a much more immersive video/ call-listening/live experience environment would improve both knowledge and confidence when new staff go live. New staff should have 24 hour access to a dedicated on-line training resource with short videos and podcasts covering in detail how to handle all call types and how to deal with difficult or angry customers. This aspect of the role should not be ignored and we believe that the more we expose new staff to difficult callers and offer easy to use coping and handling mechanisms the easier it will be for them to deal with such callers when they are inevitably presented with them. The real world nature of the on-line training materials would reduce the shock and discomfort suffered by trainees when they first experience nasty callers.

For any of this to be agreed and moved forward we would have to begin dialogue with all clients immediately. As the training courses as they stand are owned and managed exclusively by clients we would have to persuade them of the need to change format and involve them in sign-off for each aspect of the change. Experience tells us that clients often feel that they know best when it comes to induction training and will not submit to change easily. Negotiations around this would have to happen at the highest level and usually involve sign-off at board level.

On a purely personal level my gut feel was that the first two goals could be achieved within 7 working days – or less if we really put our minds to it. Frankly, I didn't think we'd get much movement from most of our clients on the third. In the past any such suggestions had been disregarded as they believed their complete ownership of design and style of delivery should remain 100% intact and that us taking a lead on any change was regarded as arrogance and unwanted interference. I liked the idea of an on-line training resource and felt it had promise but couldn't see our largest clients agreeing to it. However, any progress would be worthwhile but I wanted to ensure we managed everyone's expectations.

So, now we move on to Grad Bay – what could we do here to help our work in this area become more valued and respected by inductees?

Grad Bay

Having genuinely spent some time planning how to deliver the new inductees' feedback to the team working on the Grad Bay I was disappointed with the response. For the most part it wasn't accepted as genuine and minds were closed to possible improvements almost straight away. Others simply walked away citing 'ingratitude' and 'not being valued' as their reasons for withdrawing from these opportunities which, just a few weeks earlier, had been perceived as a chance to demonstrate to decision makers that these guys were just about ready to be considered for more senior roles. I know this isn't a good thing to admit as it's pretty petty but frankly those who walked away put themselves at the bottom of the list for any future promotions until they had proved me wrong about them. Toys out the pram is never a good look and something I can't get past when it comes to assessing individuals for more senior jobs.

Those who were prepared to stay and listen, however, began to take on board how new trainees had felt about their interaction with the group and started to think about how they could make essential improvements.

First they had to analyse the criticism and break it down into the key areas that had to be altered or re-invented. Next, they should look again at the advisers selected to work on Grad Bay. Were they the 'right' type of people to support brand new people, just in the door and who were terrified of what they were being asked to do for the first time. Had we, yet again, selected on competence in the adviser role rather than on settling for lesser competence but focussing on empathy and emotional intelligence. Could we find a group of guys who would be naturally focussed on best supporting our newest people rather than simply acting as expert advisers keen to show of their system and product knowledge but less disposed to making a nervous individual feel a little bit better about him or herself? And finally, how could Grad Bay better place itself as subject matter expert fit to advise on, and improve, the work of both the Training and Operations departments without stepping on their toes or overstepping the mark? Not an easy task given the prima donna style sensitivities prevalent amongst the decision makers in both of these areas. Anyway, these questions became the basis of their objectives as part of this exercise.

So, here are the initial objectives accepted by the small group of people tasked to manage the Grad Bay and the individuals seconded to it:

Short Term Goal:

Utilising support from IT and Management Information teams, analyse the detailed feedback from questionnaires completed by the last two hundred new employees to pass through their hands. Using a basic 80/20 approach firm up on the five most common areas of criticism and produce a plan of action to eliminate these specific concerns across the next six months.

Medium Term Goal:

Using the above feedback form a very clear view on how suitable each member of the the Grad Bay seconded team is to the role. Give the poorest performers the opportunity to re-train or step away while creating a new role description to help recruit the newest members of the support team with the emphasis on emotional intelligence. Build and begin to deliver a short training course designed to cover the nature of the feedback received from from recent 'graduates' together with instruction on how best to meet both the needs of the business and the aspirations of new trainees.

Long Term Goal:

Work with Training and Operations to create a mechanism where Grad Bay feedback can formally inform induction content and support Operations and Planning in identifying where positive relationships had developed between new staff that could be sustained by keeping people connected within their new teams and shifts.

Finally...Operations. What should they be focussing on to help reduce staff attrition and make the organisation more attractive to new staff? I think the answers were pretty obvious as annual staff satisfaction surveys had been highlighting the same issues for a few years. To cut a long story short, the three complaints which were consistently being raised were lack of family friendly shifts, unsupportive management culture and lack of opportunities to develop skills and move into other, more technical roles. These are all big issues and finding solutions will rely on support from Planning, Finance, HR, Training and just about every other function within the business. Sticking to the Short, Medium, Long Term objectives model was adhered to but I believe everyone understood that things like changing the management culture could take years and that a glib attempt to achieve it in 3 or 6 months would be futile. Anyway, we continued to use the simplified system for consistency sake.

Short Term Goal:

Acknowledge to all staff that agent and team manager shifts were currently not fully supportive of family and social life and also that the hybrid model of working from home as well as the office had been relatively successful during lockdown and that the business was now committed to finding solutions that worked for everyone. It should be understood that shift inefficiency can be very costly if it means bringing in large numbers of new staff to compensate for making existing shifts more user-friendly but every effort would be made to find a suitable halfway house that would make life more comfortable for all existing staff and help to recruit new people too.

Work closely with HR, Planning and Finance to develop a new homeworking/family friendly shift model and roll out within 12 months.

Medium Term Goal:

Work with all other functions to identify opportunities to develop into viable support for other areas of the business. Recruitment, HR, Training, Finance, IT, Planning should – where possible – be looking to recruit new staff from within the existing workforce. Ops managers should identify potential talent and obvious ambition within their groups and support these individuals along formal pathways to shadowing and sufficient skills development that would permit people from within the current agent community to authentically apply for other internal roles and be seriously considered by the recruiting function. Massively important that this doesn't become simply a paper exercise where no-one is genuinely expected to make these kinds of moves due to lack of relevant knowledge or experience. We must provide the knowledge and some of the experience.

Agent ambitions must become a significant part of performance management strategies and form part of annual objective setting and monthly 121 reviews.

Senior Operations Managers should work with all function heads to provide a mini route to competence for each skillset. Shadowing is inexpensive as long as the agent commits to giving up some of their spare time to do it while knowledge can be shared through password protected elements of the company intranet site. Relationships with local colleges should be developed to help us support our best and most ambitious people into further education. Successes should be celebrated both internally and in the local media.

Long Term Goal:

This is the hard one – how do you go about re-inventing a management culture within an organisation made up of two thousand people with a couple of hundred managers already firmly set in their ways?

To keep things very short (a very long book could be written on this topic alone) it comes from the top. The business has to decide what its core values are and every member of staff should be recruited, trained and managed on the basis of these values. Poor behaviours should be identified and dealt with while training on a more emotionally intelligent, supportive, coaching style of management should be rolled out with immediate effect. Future recruitment of managers should focus on personal characteristics rather than simple skills-related competence. Everyone joining in a management role should fit the personality model pre-determined by senior management while staff should be encouraged to identify any outliers in terms of poor performance or attitude to allow reviews to take place and any adjustments made...bear in mind there's always two sides to every story and one man's idea of aggression or insensitivity may simply be another's idea of discipline and determination. We do not want to irritate the existing management teams by implying that they are currently incompetent.

Informally collect feedback from all staff to be delivered to their line manager at 121s and focus on scoring how managers are viewed as part of annual Staff Satisfaction Survey.

Reward managers who most meet the new management style criteria.

Chapter 8

It has been eighteen months since we kicked off on our Recruitment and Retention Improvement Plan – more than enough time to evaluate any positive impacts that may have resulted from our actions. Like all extensive plans of this kind it's important to understand that positive change happens incrementally and not in a blinding flash of instant success. The results of our plan and subsequent activity are no different and we are all too aware that it's very much how we react to the outcomes we've seen that will determine whether we have done the right things and made the kind of progress we had hoped for.

I won't sugar coat our outcomes. Some have been noticeable and pleasing while others were a disappointment and , frankly, feel like a little bit of a waste of effort. I'm not convinced that all of our responsible staff were equally committed to driving gains and I now have a slightly tainted view of the motives and application levels of some of our people. However, some of the things we did proved to be worthwhile and worth celebrating and building upon.

Anyway, here are my observations on how things turned out split by Recruitment and Retention based on where I feel the impacts most lie.

Staff Recruitment

The new manager we employed rejuvenated the team bringing new energy and ambition so this was a major – if unplanned for – win. She ignored or dealt with historical challenges and uncertainties and appeared to make progress where previously it had seemed impossible.

The most obvious success was the set up of a 'bank' approach to recruitment whereby we recruited regularly every month irrespective of whether we had any current vacancies or not. Through redesigning how we advertised the roles and making our business appear to be the destination of choice for all aspiring customer service agents and those currently working for competitor organisations in our locality. We made it clear when no roles were immediately available but we also treated any successful candidates like rock stars to help them feel that, no matter when the call actually came to join us for real, they were joining somewhere special and that a short wait for the right job to come up was a small price to pay.

We sent them a newsletter every month by email, invited them in for lunch with senior staff and, where possible, kept them fully informed on when CSA roles were going to start and the date on which induction training would begin. Staff from our Recruitment team became their buddies within our business, keeping them fully informed on everything positive happening within the business. Needless to say we had some negative reactions to this and a small number of potential new recruits got fed up with the wait and accused us of stringing them along – in spite of us being 100% clear throughout the process that a wait of a few months was possible. In the end our average wait was six weeks as we had a constant pipeline of new business and backfill training calendar on-going throughout the year. Planning our recruitment on this basis meant that we were able to give successful candidates up to four weeks' notice that they would be joining us which allowed for people in existing roles elsewhere to tell their current employers that they would be leaving and were able to work their notice of termination according to their contracts. This means that they left on the best possible terms and other employers could not accuse us of forcing their leavers to join us without working their statutory notice period.

Looking back from this point some 18 months since the initiative began I think we can claim this initiative has been a success. It has provided us with an average of 3.7 FTE per induction training group of 15 FTE – all of whom were well aware of the nature of both the role and our business. Importantly, attrition (leavers percentage) for this group, measured on a 12 month moving average basis is just 22% compared to close to 80% (yes!!! 8 out of 10 people were leaving in less than 12 months) when you look at the CSA community as a whole. Also, we've seen some of the early recruits from this bank approach beginning to move into other roles and could well be some of the people who take our business forward in the coming years.

It has required a great deal of persistent ambition and energy but the bank approach has worked for us.

Next, our Recruitment team looked at a different model of recruiting based on selecting new recruits based on attitude and personal characteristics rather then simply semi-relevant experience. In the past, if you'd worked in customer service in an electrical superstore at weekends when you were at school ten years ago then you had a 95% chance of being offered a CSA role with us irrespective of what the rest of your life looked like. So, a new employee could be a useless nightmare to work with but we would never have done the kind of digging that would have identified that simply because the applicant had some previous half-relevant experience.

After some analysis of our existing staff and their backgrounds we discovered that many – if not most – of our best current CSAs did not have much in the way of relevant experience but their CVs and behaviours and habits having joined us clearly outlined that they had a history of committing themselves to an organisation or hobby or family related service and sustaining that over a period of time. In simplistic terms, if an applicant had a longish record of, for example, managing a Scout group every Tuesday and Thursday evening together with volunteering for camps each Summer then they were more likely to ride the ups and downs of training for work in a contact centre and pursuing something resembling a career once their feet were under the table. This equally applied to regular charity workers, sports people, musicians, amateur dramatists, Girl Guide leaders and those studying in their own time for recognised qualifications etc.

So, we decided to create a hybrid selection model where both experience and characteristics demonstrating sustained commitment to an organisation or cause other than themselves. This had to be a positive step as the existing model wasn't working for us and distinct improvements had to be made. In the end, rather that reinventing the wheel, we decided to use an outside, third party supplier to help us both create the new model but also to train our Recruitment team members in how to use it.

Now, as you can imagine, this didn't come cheap and some of our most senior people were concerned that we would be laying out thousands of pounds with no guarantees that the new system and process would improve the standard of successful applicant and reduce our numbers of leavers. A detailed cost/benefit analysis was put together and we managed to find a company that had some experience in this space and was prepared to accept a partial risk/reward approach to payment meaning that they would be paid in part for the success of the process measured across a twelve month period alongside an agreement that we would give them more training-related business should this exercise prove a success.

Looking back we were a little naïve. Initially we didn't attract sufficient numbers of suitable applicants to make this approach worthwhile and had to make adjustments to our recruitment advertising to stimulate applications from the 'new' type of interested party we were keen to encourage. Now, one thing our third-party partner had failed to warn us about – I reckon we could have worked this out for ourselves mind you – was that applicants with regular and sustained commitments to charities, clubs, bands, amateur operatic societies and Girl Guides etc. would want to continue these associations and would require regular time off and appropriate shift patterns to allow them to attend meetings, training, rehearsals as normal.

As we began to attract this king of applicant in decent numbers our Recruitment team began to tear their collective hair out as we were simply unable to offer new people a shift pattern that meant they could finish at 6pm on two nights of the week and have every Sunday off. If we had offered these shifts to new guys our existing people would have been, quite rightly, up in arms and we would, without doubt, have lost some of our best people. Some applicants were already working in roles which offered them the shifts they required and simply weren't prepared to move jobs and lose the shift guarantee. In fact, for some of them, their spare time activities were their top priority and work had to fit around those rather than the other way around. So, while we were beginning to attract the kind of applicant we wanted we had to knock them back almost immediately. Our partner training company people were getting pretty annoyed with us too. After all, they told us they could help us attract the right kind of applicant, had proved that their methods worked then discovered we were knocking back 90% of them as we couldn't accommodate their shift requirements. Some very heated reviews took place across the first six months of the exercise.

In the end we had to compromise and focus on people for whom fixed times and days off were not an absolute requirement and we managed to find ways to support the more flexible of that community through use of planned rota'd days off, shift swaps etc.

So, looking back across the last eighteen months, the exercise has worked in that we have attracted more of the 'committed' types but not in the numbers we had hoped for. Resource planning for these guys has been a bit of a nightmare and some existing staff have raised concerns that they believed we were doing more to accommodate untested new people rather than rewarding the best performing current staff members who had, for some time, been looking for improved shifts. Of course they were right and we have had to formalise how we reward our best people in terms of putting together more family friendly rotas and delivering for these very important people.

The three short recruitment videos we made were definitely a success. They proved helpful in that no-one could reach telephone interview stage until they had watched the short films, read the interviews with existing staff and established a very clear picture of the kinds of people who joined us as CSAs and what the job looked and felt like. If we interviewed anyone who couldn't answer the simple questions we asked them about our recruitment website content they were politely informed that we had expected more commitment from all applicants and perhaps they should think again about whether they really wanted to work with us. Needless to say we took some flack for this approach on social media but I was happy about the message it delivered to the community of people who were considering working with us: prepare properly and have a clear view of the role you're applying for or don't bother contacting us.

The films were made by two smart people from within our IT team who had made promotional videos for local bands in the past and really knew what they were about. We asked for volunteers from the floor to share their stories on camera and allow us to use them on our new dedicated jobs website which was linked from our main corporate internet presence. We asked our people to tell us about how they found out about the organisation, what the recruitment process was like, their experience of induction training and the terrifying prospect of going live. They then offered a view on how they felt about their role and the company now they they were established and, finally, advice to anyone thinking of applying for the agent positions we had been advertising.

Disappointingly we didn't get too many volunteers to begin with. In fact, the only people happy to help out were the usual selection of hard-working, well-intentioned employees intent on making a name for themselves in order to further their careers. I was happy that one of our videos should include someone from this group but not all. It had to be as 'real' as possible to be worthwhile and I wanted to hear from conflicted staff who had not had the smoothest of times but had persevered and found the outcome to be worthwhile. So, we asked our most influential of managers to get out amongst their guys and find us five people with great stories to tell. I wanted the truth – it was important they didn't hold back of any criticisms they had and they needed to be able to explain, in their own words, how they felt about customers – especially the challenging ones – and dealing with other staff within our business. It was massively important that any applicant watching the films came away with a very transparent notion of what the day-to-day job looked and felt like...warts and all.

We needed the five volunteers to be of differing backgrounds, age, sex, experience etc. so that anyone watching the films would have a good chance of spotting someone a bit like themselves. In the end we got them. Two eventually said that they didn't want their films to go up on the website but were happy to be quoted – first names only – as part of a transcribed interview. The other three gave us more or less what we wanted so our IT guys got to work and created some very slick output – even using licence free music from their contacts in local bands to support the action.

So, we got a young college leaver doing their first ever full-time job, a single mum who worked with us part-time as she needed to balance her hours with looking after the kids and a man of nearly sixty who had recently retired from the police but was too energetic to sit at home behaving like the archetypal pensioner. Each told the viewer a little bit about their background, how they found induction and going live and a little bit about dealing with the challenges of the role. We had to ensure that anyone viewing would get the clearest picture of what the job looked and felt like with almost no holds barred. We didn't sugar-coat anything but, it must be said, we didn't include anything too negative or disparaging as this would probably have deterred most new applicants.

What we did do was show our people handling difficult customers then talking about the experience immediately after. It was crucial that all applicants understood the stresses and strains of the day-to-day before coming to speak to us about employment. The films, together with the other interview transcriptions, presented a pretty accurate picture of how some of our people feel about working with us in a CSA role. This stimulated a number of searching questions from applicants at interview but it was imperative that everyone understood that customer service meant dealing with all customers and not just the ones we liked. It was imperative that no-one should join us then leave within three months claiming they didn't have a realistic view of what the job entailed – especially around having to deal with unpleasant people and to what extent our shift patterns impacted on trying to achieve a perfect work/life balance. We all have to face up to the facts of contact centre life which are the acceptance of the nature of the work, unpleasant callers are now as common as pleasant ones and that being open seven days a week for 14 hours per day means that inconvenient shift rotations are inevitable. Frankly, anyone who can't accept these things really should not be working in our kind of environment.

Happily, most successful applicants later told us that the films had been useful if not 100% accurate in their portrayal of the stresses of the job and I firmly believe that they prevented some people joining us who simply wouldn't have been up to the task and who would have caused us headaches and cost us money. The site has to be regularly updated and new videos included to keep things fresh, reflect feedback from viewers and replace any member of staff who may have left us.

Finally in the recruitment space I believe we improved communications between the dedicated Recruitment team and both the Training and Grad Bay functions. Monthly reviews allowed all three groups to compare notes on successes and failures with each member of every new intake being discussed and views taken on whether the individuals concerned had been good recruits or otherwise. Occasionally this meant going right back to first and second interview notes to try to understand how someone who didn't fit managed to get through our process. We also got together the guys in Operations with Recruitment who had expressed an interested in roles in that space. They went on to shadow existing Recruitment staff and supported in the admin tasks when new intakes took place meaning they learned the challenges of handling visas and references which ae always a hassle frankly when new people have to be employed quickly.

Training

Our Training people quickly got their act together too putting a major focus on redesigning existing induction courses to support our new intentions around concentrating on the five most common enquiry/call types which represented 80% of our traffic. The other 20% would still be covered but our plan was to support these contact types during Grad Bay whilst allowing new people to go live able to deal with the majority of common call types with the minimum of support. A couple of our clients were a little slow to get on board with this but we promised them an immediate reversion to the previous content if we found our experiment unsuccessful after six months. In fact it proved a universal success with new people more confident from their first day live and clients used our experience to flavour some of their induction processes going forward.

We also redesigned the method of training delivery to move away from presentation based classroom activity to something more akin to call listening or enquiry handling interactions by contact type, role play and floor buddying. I make no apologies for saying this again – most of the people who come to us for CSA jobs did not learn well in classes at school so we have to alter our teaching style to reflect how they best learn. This means dropping a lot of the presentation based stuff and replacing it with some much more interactive. Doing this also means that going live is much less of a scary experience as they'll have experienced literally hundreds of contacts and responses prior to their first day on their own in front of screens or on the phones. Proper planning alongside Operations and Resource Planning meant that all new trainees were buddied with keen, enthusiastic and engaged existing CSAs who were only too keen to pass on their knowledge and experience to newbies. Needless to say this proved less than perfect due to some agents going a little rogue in terms of their behaviours but we'd planned for this...I've been doing this a long time and know that some people will always take the opportunity to lash out at management if they've experienced something negative within the recent past. Anyone who has been turned down for leave they really wanted or failed to win promotion will make sure they inform new staff of their somewhat tainted view of the organisation at the first available opportunity.

   Working alongside our IT people Training designed and created content for a dedicated, password protected element of our intranet where trainees could listen to calls of all types (private data removed obviously) and see all forms of digital enquiry followed by a complete breakdown of how best to respond and where to find the information to allow them to respond correctly. Perfect example calls were included alongside short video demonstrations of how to handle the five most common types of calls together with a checklist of what to include in every contact response allowing new people to build their own call structure that suits their personality...within given guidelines of course.

Operations

Not to be outdone by the previous two functions, Operations quickly got their act together too. First they worked with Resource Planning and Finance to create a staffing model which would support revised 'family-friendly' shift rotas which would create a better work/life balance for our people but not be so inefficient that it cost the business a fortune. More part-time opportunities, three day 12 hour shifts and a move away from the standard 37.5 hours per week requirement were all considered and integrated into our updated thinking on planning. Not easy at all but we came up with some hybrid experiments that proved both popular and effective. A challenge for Recruitment certainly but we did begin to make a name for ourselves in terms of offering something different to the local workforce.

Ops also worked hard on putting together a hybrid home worker/office-based employee model to offer successful, experienced people. We had loads of experience from lockdown times when just about everyone worked from home but we had to come up with something cost-effective that rewarded our best people as this level of flexibility is the price businesses of this kind are going to have to learn to pay for attracting good people to work in CSA roles as we move forward. We had the equipment and the know-how so it was hard to see why we couldn't run a couple of pilots to test how effective home-working could be in a time when Covid wasn't the driver. As usual I'm sure you can take guess at the outcomes of these pilots – it was great for some people and less so for others. The challenge would be selecting those who could work well independently without disappointing those who clearly could not. But, at least we had on offer that some of our best people could aspire to while educating others that handling calls at home during fixed working times cannot run alongside the childcare of two under fives!! One had to displace the other by necessity. A redesign of management practices was also required to support the new hybrid model.

A revitalised approach to Grad Bay was also part of the Ops remit and they did this by going through a new streamlined selection and training process where empathy and emotional intelligence was put at the heart of every action and reaction. It was crucial to fill the Grad Bay team with people whose first instinct was to get off their backsides and genuinely help the struggling new people rather than sit detached at a group of desks with their mates scrolling on the internet and ignoring the hands of panicked newbies becoming increasingly desperate in the pods behind them. Of course this meant disappointing some of the existing support team and temporarily blunting the ambition of others who believed their relative experience of call-handling entitled them to move to nursery support immediately the positions became available. I'm sure we lost a couple of these disappointed staff when they saw their route to promotion blocked but were they such a great loss when we already knew that they would not be suitable for a move to the next rung of the ladder? A loss of an experienced agent certainly is diluting the experience pool by replacing experienced staff with inexperienced people and is never a strong way ahead but not a problem in terms of finding future leaders and, more importantly, capable Grad Bay support staff.

Chapter 9

So, in conclusion, what can I advise based on almost two years of virtually reinventing our approach to recruitment and staff retention? What is worthwhile attempting and what is not?

First, let's look at the priorities of the kind of people we're trying to recruit and hang on to as defined by the research conducted by almost every employment agency you can engage with via the internet. They all tell us the same thing in that, post lockdown, we will have to fight harder to recruit good people than ever before and we must make changes if we want to be successful. It's commonly felt that the new aspiring CSR's priorities are something like:

1. Fair pay
2. Family-friendly shifts
3. Comprehensive training
4. Development opportunities
5. Emotionally intelligent management community
6. Company ethos reflecting inclusiveness and community focus

Needless to say, if you manage to do well in each of these areas and communicate this in every aspect of what you do then you're going to do pretty well for yourselves. However, each of these things is expensive and challenging to deliver day in and day out with very few failures. I don't know of anyone who consistently achieves the highest standards in respect of all of the above. I believe that our organisation have had a terrific attempt at it and most of the successes and failures are pretty obvious for all to see. We did, though, see a marked improvement in retention numbers after 18 months. Volume recruitment became harder due to the constraints we put in place around prescribed character type, real-life videos demonstrating the challenges of the role and recruiting ahead of actual planned induction training intakes but the people we got in were better prepared for what was coming and had the necessary personal characteristics to allow them to deal with the inevitable ups and downs.

Anyway, after 18 months our annualised attrition rate across our three biggest campaigns stood at 38% against our starting point of approximately 80%. We also were able to retain an average of 86% of recent trainees compared to just 66% at the beginning of the exercise.

Also, a significant improvement in ratings and feedback was observed as part of our annual employee engagement survey. We delayed the survey till 9 months into the new plan to see if our efforts were being appreciated and it seems that they were.

Sadly, it's much more difficult to put together an accurate picture of cost savings versus increases in costs caused by paying the living wage, new shift patterns, the expense of purchasing the latest IT equipment to support home-working and having to use agency staff when we couldn't recruit in the volumes we had previously achieved due to stricter criteria. However, it's safe to say that we didn't have to replace the 200 or so leavers we would have expected to under the previous regime so that could estimated saving of around £400k which is considerably more than I believe would have been our increased costs. A strong experience pool was maintained as opposed to having to constantly add high numbers of new people into the system every month which was a win for both our clients and their customers' experience of dealing with us. I perceived an improved relationship between our business and our key clients due to the higher standards of service delivery we were able to offer. I can't report too many negatives other than the disruption caused by the necessary truth-telling at the start of the exercise. Some egos were severely damaged and relationships stretched to the max.

So, in the end, in my view what was worth doing and what was a waste of time?

All of the recruitment changes were worth making. Each of them meant better quality, better- prepared people were delivered to training ahead of induction and I don't regret any of it. However, if you are in a position where you need to recruit 100 new people every month for six months you're going to have to relax some of your standards if you are to fill these requisitions. It is not possible to find large numbers of really good people (according to our new criteria) in such a short period of time. Many will not have the required staying power characteristics you've been looking for and some will join you, ignoring the real-world video examples, convincing themselves to take the job for a few weeks to get their families and government agencies off their backs in the full knowledge that they won't be able to handle the challenges and complexities of the role long-term.

Well-advertised, communicated, celebrated and supported business in the community type days can make all the difference when helping people feel good about who they work for. If you are going to go to the expense of giving all staff one day off to support a local cause then at least take the time to organise the days well and make then count for something both inside and outside of the business.

It goes without saying that paying at least the living wage gives new recruits and existing staff alike the dignity of feeling they are being decently rewarded and that they work for a considerate employer.

If I can advise you to do just one thing it would be to move your classroom based induction training to something much more hands-on. Lots of call listening, role playing, buddying and interactive 'fun' will produce more confident trainees at the end of the initial course. Your new people – on the whole – will not react well to presentation style training so change the style as soon as you can and include 30 mins catch-up at the end of every Grad Bay day to cover off the real-world challenges they experience. Do a basic Pareto analysis and focus on the call or enquiry types that represent 80% of your traffic the rest will develop as a matter of course. Videos and recordings people can access will allow them to familiarise themselves with what they are going to be dealing with in their own time and takes away the scary uncertainty of what they will be exposed to when they go live. The more live calls they hear in training the better prepared they'll be for going live.

Better shifts and a hybrid home/office approach to call or enquiry handling are a must in the modern day. Almost everyone wants the chance to work from home and you have to be able to offer that to the appropriate staff and the people who manage them. Fail to do this and you'll fall behind your competitors. Most of us made it work during lockdown so why can't we do it now?

So there you have it. Almost all of it is basic common sense and, for all I know, you may be doing some or all of these things already but could they do with a fresh approach? All I know is that what we attempted to achieve brought good results and shook up the complacency of some of the key parts of our business while, in the end, driving cost savings and improving employee engagement. Not a bad result at all.

www.ingramcontent.com/pod-product-compliance
Lightning Source LLC
Chambersburg PA
CBHW071834210526
45479CB00001B/138